DIVINITY
& DIVERSITY

A CHRISTIAN AFFIRMATION
OF RELIGIOUS PLURALISM

MARJORIE HEWITT SUCHOCKI

Abingdon Press
Nashville

DIVINITY AND DIVERSITY
A CHRISTIAN AFFIRMATION OF RELIGIOUS PLURALISM

Library of Congress Cataloging-in-Publication Data

Suchocki, Marjorie.
    Divinity and diversity : a Christian affirmation of religious pluralism / Marjorie Hewitt Suchocki.
        p. cm.
    ISBN 0-687-02194-4 (pbk.   :   alk. paper)
    1. Christianity and other religions. 2.   Religious pluralism—Christianity.   I. Title.

BR127.S88 2003
261.2—dc21

                                                                    2003001114

Scripture quotations, unless otherwise noted are taken from the NEW AMERICAN STANDARD BIBLE®, Copyright © 1960, 1962, 1963, 1968, 1971, 1972, 1973, 1975, 1977, 1995 by The Lockman Foundation. Used by permission.

Scripture marked ASV is from the American Standard Version of the Bible.

Scripture marked KJV is from the King James Version of the Bible.

Scripture marked TANAKH is from The TANAKH: The New JPS Translation According to the Traditional Hebrew Text. Copyright 1985 by the Jewish Publication Society. Used by permission.

Portions of chapter 3 were originally published in Religion in a Pluralistic Age: Proceedings of the Third International Conference on Philosophical Theology, edited by Donald A. Crosby and Charley D. Hardwick. Copyright 2001, Peter Lang Publishing, Inc., New York. Material is used with permission of the publisher.

06 07 — 10 9 8 7 6 5 4

MANUFACTURED IN THE UNITED STATES OF AMERICA

DIVINITY
& DIVERSITY

Dedicated with Grateful Appreciation
to
The Credo Group
of Marvin United Methodist Church
Tyler, Texas

CONTENTS

PREFACE

In the not-so-distant American past, small-town Protestants might have defined religious pluralism as Methodist, Baptist, and Presbyterian churches all in the same town. At the edges of consciousness (if not the edges of town) there were Roman Catholics, too—and perhaps Jews. Urban Protestants might have been more forthright in their recognition of a common Christianity that included Protestants and Catholics together, but a major issue in pluralism was how Christian churches related to one another. Ecumenism was the growing edge of religious practice, and ministerial associations developed as ways to understand one another and cooperate with one another. Insofar as Christians recognized pluralism as involving religions other than Christianity, Judaism was often the only candidate in town—and often Judaism was swept into the Christian circle as a distant older sibling of Christianity.

Religious pluralism as we know it today radically undercuts those assumptions, for virtually every town in America is living space for a variety of religions. Hindu temples are raised, Buddhists meet in sanghas, Muslims build mosques. Worldwide immigration and emigration patterns mean that persons from religions other than one's own are now neighbors. Furthermore, through marriage or conversion, persons from religions other than one's own are often family!

How do Christians deal with this phenomenon? Our Christian past has traditionally taught us that there is only one way to God, and that is through Christ. But we are uneasy. Our neighborliness teaches us that these others are good and decent people, good neighbors, or loved family members! Surely God is with them as well as with us. Our hearts reach out, but our intellectual understanding draws back. We have been given little theological foundation for affirming these others—and consequently, we wonder if our feelings of acceptance are perhaps against the will of God, who has uniquely revealed to us just what is required for salvation.

"New occasions teach new duties," is a line from a hymn. But new occasions may also teach new ways of thinking. This book explores new ways of thinking about old Christian doctrines, exploring them for new insights into religious pluralism. In the first chapter I set out the problem of religious pluralism. The second chapter, "Creation," is based on God's transcendence, especially as witnessed in Genesis 1. God creates through "call and response," with each new call being based on the world's previous response. Such a creation, I argue, requires pluralism as a witness to God's work *with* the world, rather than somehow *on* the world independent of its response.

The third chapter, "Radical Incarnation," is based on God's immanence. Insofar as God's call is taken into the becoming world, God is incarnate in the world. God is at work within religions—all religions, not just our own. The fourth chapter, "The Image of God," is based on Trinitarian theology. "Trinity" names God as an irreducible diversity existing in the unity of divine love. Further, the internal love of God is expressed externally through calling into being that which is most deeply other to God, the creature. If God calls us to be God's own image, then we too must learn to love not only within the internal diversity of our various modes of Christianity, but beyond ourselves toward the deeper diversity of religious pluralism. The Reign of God provides my fourth symbol. A mark of God's reign is our treatment of the "stranger within our gates." We are to care for the well-being of the stranger. In today's world, the "strangers within our gates" are the persons from different religious traditions.

To call upon these four Christian doctrines/symbols to justify an affirmation of religions other than Christianity calls for exploration of what we mean by salvation in Jesus Christ. This topic is explored in chapter 6, "Saving Grace." And finally, the issue of mission is considered in chapter 7. It may seem paradoxical to say that mission is more important, not less important, in a religiously diverse world. But if God is calling us to new modes of friendship, this cannot be accomplished apart from mission.

Friendship requires forthrightness about who we are, and an eagerness to listen to who the other is. Friendship requires knowing one another, which requires witnessing to one another about our experiences, our beliefs. And friendship involves us in working together for the common good of a world of peace, of sustainable lifestyles, of care for the planet and all its inhabitants. Friendship cannot happen by withdrawal into our tightly drawn circles; we must go forth, reach out, in love of God and neighbor.

My conviction in writing this book is that God is calling religious peoples in particular to model new ways of friendship in today's world. We can no longer afford our wars—if ever we could!—and we only increase the horror and shame when we name our religions as reasons for war. I believe God calls us to a "peaceable kingdom" of God's reign in this world. That reign will be a reflection of God's image through the emerging creation of the world as a community of many communities, where we each learn to respect one another and work with one another in friendship.

ACKNOWLEDGMENTS

Many communities have helped me in preparing this book. First, I must name The University of Manchester, England, which graciously invited me to deliver the Ferguson Lectures in March 2000. Those four lectures became the nucleus of what is now Divinity and Diversity. Likewise I thank the Fresno Interfaith Council for hearing rudimentary versions of these lectures, also in 2000. Two other schools also heard various lectures based on the topic in 2001: Graceland University in Lamoni, Iowa, and Millsaps College in Jackson, Mississippi. Also in 2001 the Foundation for Christian Theology in Houston, Texas, heard versions of the fourth and fifth chapters. The animated questions and discussions from each of these groups were fruitful and challenging as I continued to probe this subject. The deep interest evoked by the topic convinced me even more that our converging world demands sustained Christian reflection on how we regard other religions. Given the tragic drama of September 11, we now know that we must learn how to understand one another and get along with one another or suffer terrible consequences.

I am grateful to my faculty colleagues at Claremont School of Theology for listening to my musings on Christian pluralism and guiding me to various resources. In particular, I'm glad to name Kathy Black, Elizabeth Conde-Frazier, Jack Coogan, and Greg Riley. And I thank Professor Darby Ray of Millsaps College for her spirited participation in naming this book.

Finally, I name the group to whom this book is dedicated: the phenomenal Credo Group at Marvin United Methodist Church in Tyler, Texas. This group first contacted me in 1999, while I was a visiting professor at Vanderbilt Divinity School. "Did I ever come to churches?" they wondered. My fervent desire has been to see an increasing number of laity theologically attuned to the great issues of our day, and engaged in probing, discussing, and developing theological understanding. Delighted with the invitation, I eagerly accepted, and so began what is now a continuing dialogue with this amazing group of Christians. From various walks of life, each member brings Christian commitment and curiosity to their joint task of deepening their understandings of Christian faith. They study theology, history, and biblical studies with zest, delighting as much in their disagreements as their agreements. They were the first to hear and respond to very early drafts of what is now this book. With gratitude I dedicate this book to them, with the old blessing: "May your tribe increase!"

CHAPTER ONE

THE TASK

I t is my purpose to affirm religious pluralism, and to argue that religious pluralism uniquely presents, from a Christian perspective, the opportunity and challenge for a new realization of the reign of God in human history. I emphasize that this is a Christian perspective, for there are reasons internal to Christianity to value the authenticity and saving importance of religions other than Christianity. Persons from other traditions who also move in the direction of valuing religious pluralism will look for their own internal religious reasons for doing so.

In a pluralistic universe, there is no religious equivalent to a sky-lab where we can go to escape our religious and cultural histories. There is no vantage point from outside ourselves that gives us a privileged view of the way things *really* are. The apostle Paul aptly phrased our situation thus: "Now we see through a glass, darkly" (1 Cor. 13:12 KJV). Our interpretations of this pluralism that we increasingly experience are framed from inside our own stories, and must be reckoned as such. We see God and God's ways with the world as God appears to us, not as God appears to all people at all times—much less as God appears to God! To say this, of course, immediately marks me as coming from a religion that affirms there is God, for not all religions do. Many forms of Buddhism, for example, would consider some Christian ideas of God to be a violation of a central Buddhist principle of nonduality (the interdependent unity of all things).

We cannot assume that our religious norms are universally applicable to other religions any more than we assume that the norms of other religions apply to our own. But despite all these limitations, we are nonetheless required to stretch our understanding of our own religion so that it renders a reasonable account of religious pluralism in an affirmative way. To avoid this task is to face the debilitating consequences entailed in evading the reality that there *are* a variety of religions, each of which in its own way generates a community of inclusive well-being, enriches the overall welfare of the world, and speaks to its people about that which is sacred. My Christian assumption is that God is involved in the making of religions, and that given the role of culture in religion, it is absolutely necessary that there be a variety of ways of being religious.

Christian Affirmation?

However, to suggest a Christian affirmation of religious pluralism is to go against the dominant Christian understanding, which has been remarkably negative in the two thousand years of Christian history. This negativity may be summed up in the ancient dictum of Cyprian, third-century Christian bishop, that outside the church there is no salvation. In our less restrictive modes, we Christians have viewed other religions as a prelude to Christianity. As prelude, we understood that those aspects of other religions that were most like Christianity were dim portents of their fulfillment in the Christian religion. However, insofar as we understood salvation to be available only in Jesus Christ, all persons outside of Christianity were to be evangelized.

In our worst modes, of course, we have considered persons who follow other religions to be "benighted heathen" at best, and demonic at worst, and we have done what we could to rid our planet of other religions either by conversion or destruction. Christian persecution of Jews, and the Crusades that were intended to recapture Jerusalem and stamp out Islam, might be the most egregious examples of the effects of the statement, "outside the church there is no salvation." The internal persecution of Christians by Christians in the name of "correct belief," or orthodoxy, is another example. Much tragedy, arrogance, and evil have been generated by Christian exclusivism.

However, there has been an alternative if minor strand within Christian theology that suggested God works universally and graciously throughout the world in many ways. There have been remarkable (and rare) acknowledgments of the value of other religions within Christian history. One can point to the Second Council of Nicea in 787, when it was declared that Jews who did not wish to convert to Christianity should be allowed to live openly as Jews, or to Pope Gregory VII's letter to the Muslim king of Mauritania in 1076 stating that Muslims and Christians worship the same God in different ways. The Council of Trent, in 1545, spoke of a "baptism of desire" whereby persons of goodwill who knew not the Christian gospel were nonetheless saved.[1] This position was reaffirmed in the nineteenth century, and again by Karl Rahner in the twentieth century. While none of these positions is what one might call generous relative to other religions, they are at least better than the dominant position contained in Cyprian's dictum.

In its original formulation, the targets of Cyprian's statement were Christian heretics, but it was expanded to a dogma applying to all non-Christians in general, and to non-Catholics in particular. For example, the Council of Florence in 1442 declared that those not living within the Roman Catholic Church would be condemned to hell unless converted before death. Eastern Orthodox Christians were the immediate target of this statement, but the doctrine was carried to ghoulish extremes in the Inquisition. Christians who did not conform to official doctrine were put to torture to persuade them to believe correctly and presumably escape the worse torment of eternal fire. Muslims and Jews were also targets of the Inquisition, and England, France, and Spain went so far as to expel all Jews. In doing so, of course, they expropriated all Jewish property.

The rise of Protestantism did not mitigate the low regard for other religious faiths. Luther's early openness toward Jews was quickly followed by intolerance when, to his surprise, Jews did not immediately choose to become Christians upon hearing Luther's clear exposition of the gospel. The seventeenth century saw the start of the Protestant missionary movement (by then Catholic missionaries had been evangelizing the world for at least two hundred years) for the purpose of replacing other religions with Christianity. Christianity has not been known for its openness to diverse forms of religious faith either inside or outside its borders.

Contemporary Christian Pluralism

The twentieth century saw a radical transformation in this situation. Ernst Troeltsch is a key figure, for he struggled through several decades to understand the roles of history and culture in the development of religion. He moved painfully from a view that Christianity was absolute to a view that Christianity *is* absolutely true, but only for those who follow it. The relativism thus introduced did not sit easy, and indeed, theologian Karl Barth's thundering denial tried to save Christianity by placing Jesus Christ beyond history. Theologians who, like Troeltsch, looked hard at the historical evidence strove to forge an "inclusive" view of other religions that recognized their value, but saved the primacy of Christianity by making Christ the ground of all value. Theologians such as W. E. Hocking, Hendrick Kraemer, Paul Tillich, Karl Rahner, and Hans Küng (in his early writings) worked in various ways to establish both the normativeness of Christian principles and the value of religions other than Christianity.

The last decade of the twentieth century brought the issue to fervent debate. Led by Protestant theologian John Hick and Catholic theologian Paul Knitter, a veritable bevy of theologians produced numerous books and articles struggling with the issue of pluralism. In the process, three positions—each with variations—were defined: exclusivism, which affirms the old dogma that outside the church there is no salvation; inclusivism, which affirms other religions on the basis of the hidden work of Christ within them; and pluralism, which affirms other religions as authentic ways of salvation or liberation on their own terms. Yet a fourth position emerged through the writings of process theologian John B. Cobb Jr. He argues for a radical pluralism that recognizes the irreducible differences among religions, but suggests that Christ is the Logos of God, and therefore the principle of creative transformation within all the religions. Since this principle is dynamic, always producing change, interreligious dialogue becomes a way in which the ongoing traditions encounter further possibilities for their own transformation through learning from one another.[2]

Each position has its values and its problems. Exclusivism saves the universal efficacy of salvation through Jesus Christ alone, obtained by grace through faith alone. If Christ died for the sins of the world, then no other way of salvation is needed or desired. What sense does it make to say that Jesus is one of many saviors? But countering this view is the reality that naming sin as the basic human problem is a distinctly Western perception. Many Eastern cultures name suffering, not sin, as the basic problem from which we need release, so that a "saviour from sin" is somewhat irrelevant. On what basis is one analysis to be privileged over the other? And of course there is the further issue that if one is to follow Christ's statement, "by their fruits ye shall know them" (Matt. 7:20 KJV), then there is not much ethical difference between the religions. How does one account for the beneficial effects of other religions if they are not deemed to be of God?

Inclusivism avoids some of these problems by suggesting that Christ is the one supreme savior of the world, and that this salvation is at work throughout the world, whether others know it or not. Perhaps the most famous advocate of this position was Karl Rahner. For centuries the church used the concept of "baptism by desire" to account for the salvation of persons such as the repentant thief on the cross, who died without baptism. Given the extraordinary circumstances preventing that man's actual baptism, the church taught that in the eyes of God, his desire for the salvation offered by Christ constituted "baptism by desire." Using this understanding, Rahner suggested that persons who live righteously are "anonymous Christians," with their desire for righteousness constituting a "baptism by desire." A problem, however, is that the real differences from Christianity are downplayed in this view. Righteousness is measured by Christian standards, and the particular values of the religion that differ from Christianity are irrelevant to the salvation of the individuals. Thus the affirmation of otherness is gained by somehow rendering the other compatible with Christianity, which of course eliminates the very otherness it has sought to affirm.

Pluralism avoids this problem, but encounters others. Pluralist positions do not think that Christianity is the ground for salvation within other religions; instead, they respect the differences that occur. For example, pluralists affirm ways of naming the human problem that differ from Christianity's naming of sin, and recognize that each tradition develops its own unique way of addressing the problem it names. It is not necessary that there be one universal way of defining the problem with which religions deal. Instead, other commonalities are sought. Paul Knitter argues for a common commitment to justice as the basis for interreligious dialogue and action.[3] John Hick argues that the religions are varying ways of living toward "The Real," which involves a process of changing persons from self-centeredness to other-centeredness. "The Real" cannot be named, for any name would immediately privilege one religion over the others. Christians might call "The Real" God, but "The Real" transcends all names.[4]

Problems plaguing a pluralistic approach deal primarily with the threat of relativism. If each religion's "truths" are relative to its own time and place and culture, then is there no transcendent truth by which to judge them? Hick's "The Real" offers no help, because if one can say nothing at all about "The Real" beyond the fact that it is "The Real," then it offers no criterion for judging either truth or ethical conduct. Even Hick's argument that turning from self-centeredness to other-centeredness results from orientation toward "The Real" falls short, for how do we know that "The Real" values one form of centeredness over any other? If we know nothing of "The Real," we do not know what it desires. Furthermore, Christian worship—and perhaps other forms of worship as well—is not directed toward a transcendent principle; rather, it seeks relation with an ultimate Other with whom relation is actually possible. "God" is not easily replaced by "The Real."

In a sense, Knitter's position avoids these problems of "The Real," but he does not avoid the problem of relativism. By focusing on interreligious cooperation on justice issues, questions about "truth" are left behind. In goodwill, one assumes the validity of the religions represented by one's various interreligious partners. The uneasiness that emerges centers upon the fundamental condition that each religion not only assumes, but bases its very being on, the validity of its perceptions of religious truth. If we leave disagreements aside in the interest of cooperative work together, are we really addressing the depth of the other?

John B. Cobb's position tackles the depth of differences among religions head-on. They truly *are* different not only in their understanding of what's wrong with the human condition and what should be done about it, but in their understanding of the basic nature of reality as such. For example, Christians believe in God; Buddhists do not, and in some forms of Buddhism, such as Zen, the Buddha in no way functions as a "God" figure. Both positions cannot be true at the same time. Cobb answers the problem by extending pluralism beyond religions into an ultimate pluralism within the very structure of the universe. He argues that there are two "ultimates," neither of which contradicts the other. The one ultimate is God, a principle of rightness, who is named and worshiped in a number of religions. The other ultimate is creativity—that dynamic restlessness that pervades all existence in continuously changing forms, even while creativity itself has no enduring form. Buddhists, suggests Cobb, orient themselves to something called "Emptiness," which is a way of naming formless creativity as such.

But we live in one universe, not two. How do the ultimates come together? Cobb suggests Jesus Christ reveals God as the power of creative transformation. Creative transformation is the process of integrating disparate things toward something new. In one sense it is the principle of novelty operative in the world, but Cobb goes beyond this. What we see is novelty directed toward a greater good than that which was achieved in the past. If we but look, we see this continuously in the Christ of the Gospels: the sick are healed, the dead raised, the sin-laden forgiven, and ultimately, of course, Jesus himself is raised from the dead. Christ, then, is the embodiment of creative transformation, and wherever we see creative transformation, whether in Christianity or in any other religion, we see Christ. Other religions, of course, will not name the event "Christ," but the Christian will recognize the event as Christ. At times Cobb calls Christ the principle of creative transformation, so that Christ is at work wherever transformation toward the good occurs. At other times Cobb names the embodiment of creative transformation, in whatever culture or time, as "Christ." Furthermore, as the religions enter into dialogue with one another, Christ will be at work. Each religion encounters the possibility of its own radical transformation through what it learns from the other. The embodiment of these transformations, in any religion, will be recognized by the Christian as Christ.

Surely there are strengths in this view. Differences are not glossed over, but taken seriously. A difficulty is that "Christ" has been so far removed from the historic Jesus who gives rise to the naming of Christ as to be almost unrecognizable to ordinary Christians. And have we advanced so far beyond Rahner's "anonymous Christian" if Christ, unbeknownst to the various religions, is actually the one at work at the deepest level of their being? Perhaps a way out of this would be to say that a Buddhist could equally well name the Buddha as the principle of creative transformation, and see embodiments of the Buddha in all religions, including Christianity. But the very affirmation of pluralism insists that the Buddha is not the Christ, and the Christ is not the Buddha, no matter how creatively transformative the Buddha might be. Christ does not name a principle, but a person who is uniquely Jesus.

So what are we to do then? I have sketched a number of positions on religious pluralism, valuing the importance of each, but finding none entirely satisfactory.

My goal is a Christian affirmation of our own Christian tradition *and* other traditions, living toward a vision of the world as a community of diverse communities. Toward that end, I add my own voice to this intra-Christian dialogue that raises the question of religious pluralism. I invite you to journey with me in an affirmation that religious pluralism is a positive reality, not despite the competing truth claims of the various religions, but even because of these claims. Competing truths do not necessitate the quagmire of what has been called "debilitating relativism."

In the pages to follow, you will find four Christian ingredients in the thesis that Christians should celebrate the reality of many religions: (1) a theology of creation; (2) a theology of incarnation; (3) a theology of the image of God; and (4) a theology of the reign of God. But these four chapters lead to the central question raised so well by the exclusivists: What is happening on the cross of Jesus Christ? Does religious pluralism mean that Jesus does not "save" everybody? And if other religions are valid, what happens to the historic mission of the Christian church? And so my last two chapters are "Saving Grace" and "Mission in a Pluralistic World." Throughout I will be building the notion that the peoples of the earth are being called by God to become a community of friends. Diversity, rather than being a hindrance to unity, is instead absolutely necessary for deepest community.

Questions for Reflection and Discussion

- I have named four ways of dealing with pluralism: exclusivism, inclusivism, pluralism, and transformation. All are legitimate Christian views, and I have suggested strengths and weaknesses for each. What do *you* think about these ways?

- What is the religion other than Christianity that you know best? How did you learn what you know about this religion?

- How well do you know Christianity?

- If your church has never engaged in dialogue with a different religious community, would you consider recommending this action to your church? Why or why not? Do you think that greater knowledge about another religion would change your view of Christianity's relation to other religions? Is it possible that such knowledge would change your view of Christianity? How would you feel about this?

In the beginning God created the heavens and the earth. And the earth was waste and void; and darkness was upon the face of the deep; and the Spirit of God moved upon the face of the waters.

And God said, Let there be light: and there was light.

—Gen. 1:1-3 ASV

Non-being then existed not nor being:

There was no air, nor sky that is beyond it.

What was concealed? Wherein? In whose protection?

And was there deep unfathomable water?

. . . .

Who knows for certain? Who shall here declare it?

Whence was it born, and whence came this creation?

The gods were born after this world's creation:

Then who can know from whence it has arisen?

None knoweth whence creation has arisen;

And whether he has or has not produced it:

He who surveys it in the highest heaven,

He only knows, or haply he may know not.

Rig Veda 10.1, 6-7[1]

CHAPTER TWO

CREATION

Relational Suppositions

L ike the work of John B. Cobb Jr. named in the previous chapter, my own work presupposes process-relational theology. It should not be at all surprising that a similar frame of reference can be used in quite different ways—Christianity itself shows us this! Not only do we have the great divisions of Eastern forms of Orthodoxy, and the two Western divisions of Roman Catholicism and Protestantism, but each of these contains numerous subtraditions! Yet all use the same scriptures and early historical writings. Both Cobb and I use Alfred North Whitehead's process interpretation of the world as a way to develop Christian theology. But as the Christian tradition amply illustrates, to have the same starting place is not to arrive at the same conclusions.

By process-relational theology I mean a view in which relationships to others are integral to identity, and indeed, to existence itself. Who we are depends upon our own individual creative responses to physical and psychical relationships. Our bodies are formed in and through incorporation of carbon molecules originating in distant stars; the air we breathe is itself a gift from the breaths of all who have lived before us; our health depends upon our integral and synergistic relationship with a host of microbes and cells living within us. Our spiritual lives and our whole world of meaning are formed through our creative response to a vast number of relationships, the most important of which are those closest to ourselves in terms of partnership, kinship, friendship, and colleagueship.

This is fairly easy to illustrate: Think of the person who is dearest to you in all the world. Imagine your own emotional state if that person is involved in tragedy—your own well-being is deeply affected. Alternatively, imagine your emotional state when wonderful things happen to this person: a yearned-for hope materializes; a marriage takes place; a child is born. The joy of your loved one is your own joy as well, is it not? And all's well with the world! We are creatures of relationship— not puppets, not driven by relationship, but existing in and through our own creative response to relationships in various circles of importance to us. We receive from others, integrate what we receive into ourselves, and give back of ourselves to those others and indeed, to the whole universe. This is a rhythm that happens again and again, ad infinitum, to every existing thing. We can illustrate it through human physical and psychical existence, but it is a dynamic describing all existence. It is the way of the universe.

And God, also, exists in creative response to relationships. The joys of creatures become the joys of God, and the sorrows of creatures the sorrows of God. Further, in process modes of thought, God is not just the passive participant in the life of the cosmos, but the creative lure of the whole process of existence. God offers to each element in the world a way that it might most creatively respond to the influences it receives, and the world takes that influence into itself, becoming as it will, offering the result to the universe—and also back to God. God takes the results of the world's becoming into the divine nature, there values it, integrates it judgmentally into the divine self, and on the basis of what the world is becoming and God's own character, offers a possibility back to the world for the good once again.

This is a rather brief summation of a complex system that could be argued much more technically—and indeed was, in Alfred North Whitehead's Gifford Lectures resulting in the classic 1929 text, *Process and Reality*.[2] But rather than give you the details of the system, I think it enough to give you these broad outlines for a theology of creation that requires not only physical diversity, but psychical diversity—and therefore religious diversity.

Creation Out of Chaos

So let's apply this understanding to a theology of creation, first by interpreting the classic religious text of Genesis 1, and then by weaving the text and this relational worldview together to make the case for religious diversity. Too often the majestic first chapter of Genesis has been read as a quasi-scientific text for the purpose of countering theories of evolution. However, the text can just as easily be read as congruent with contemporary theories of evolution. The text itself does not purport to be a theory of creation, whether evolutionary or otherwise. Rather, the text proclaims the praise of God as creator. Through creation, God encompasses us in our deepest beginnings, so that all our times are in God's hands.

The biblical scholarship of persons such as Jon Levenson and Rolf Knierim[3]—indeed, the plain text itself—indicates that the text can be read as a remarkable portrayal of a gradual creation out of chaos. Today we might interpret this as theistic evolution. The text begins with suggestions of chaos rather than with the notion of *creatio ex nihilo* that has often been read into the text by Christians. From an evolutionary point of view, chaos is an apt beginning. Such a situation can be one where there is no observable order of inheritance from any organized past; hence, the influence of the past on the becoming present is minimal. The slow nature of the evolutionary process is because the cumulative past makes a difference to what the present can become. In a world such as ours, weighted with enduring structures that impose their own influence on each present moment, evolution is a slow, incremental affair. Transcending the past is certainly possible, but not so easy! But in a situation where there is no discernible order, where chaos and randomness are the fundamental facts of finite existence, the influence of the past is not that of a specified structure demanding its repetition in the next moment. There is no order holding the becoming present to its dictates. Therefore, God's influence over such conditions is not blocked by a past, and divinely induced change can occur through an establishment of order out of chaos. But even under such conditions, God does not act unilaterally. The finite becoming world must respond to God if God's call is to be enacted.

And the Genesis 1 text suggests just such a situation. God broods over the chaos, then gives a command: "Let there be light." Creation is through a word, a call, a lure toward a particular form of becoming.

Creation responds. There is light. The light is itself an introduction of difference and therefore definition into the chaos. If there is "light" and "dark" then there is a form of order. Insofar as the becoming world responds to the lure of "lightness," the possibility of lightness begins to become embodied, creating a structured past that now adds its own influence to that of God's call to the successor moments. It is like the dawn of creation, with light intensifying in continuous response to God's call.

C. S. Lewis's children's story, *The Magician's Nephew*,[4] gives a memorable image of God's creating power. The Lion, Aslan, is Lewis's symbol of the Word of God. A child who has fallen into the newly beginning universe of Narnia hears a voice singing in the darkness; it is the Lion, singing creation into being. The child watches and listens in awe, for the form of the Lion becomes slowly visible in the newly dawning light. As the long, continuous note of the song resounds, the light grows, until finally the full light of day has appeared. Even so in Genesis 1: God calls, and the world responds by becoming itself. And awesomely enough, in becoming itself, a trace of God becomes visible. God is a God who has valued *this* form of order, called *this* structure of being into existence.

Creation As Call and Response

But the texts offer even more. God calls, and the world responds, but then God responds to the world with judgment, valuation: "And God saw that the light was good." This is no "clock maker" deistic God, impassively spinning a world into space. Instead we have a God who evaluates and responds to the world actively in each moment, building on just this earthly response with the next divine action. The text portrays a responsive God interacting with a responsive world. God calls the world into being, and the world's order exists in and through its response to God.

God responds to the world, evaluating and integrating what the world has done with the last call into the divine self. God then calls a new form into existence, with this new form made possible by the last response. The world, shaped by its immediate ordered past and by the new call of God, responds again, becoming itself anew, and God again responds to the world's response. The God of Genesis is a God for whom the act of creating is itself a kind of covenant; it is creation through call and response.

Note also the progressive nature of the text. The sequencing of events is intentional, for each action builds toward the possibility of the next. Light, dark, and a world of ocean and dry land is necessary for the possibility of vegetation, and vegetation is necessary for the possibility of animal life, and animal life is necessary for the possibility of human life. This is not an "all at once" creation; it is progressive, with the cumulative past providing the ever-new context in which the next stage of call and response can occur. God's call depends upon creaturely response, and on the divine response to what the creature has done with the divine call. Given "that," "this" is now possible. This is theistic evolution.

Notice that both the Genesis text and the process lens through which we read the text presuppose an element of freedom in creation. The development of order, of creation rather than chaos, depends upon two types of response. On the one hand, the world must respond to God if creation is to occur. But in order for the world to become, rather than to remain a chaotic swirl of nothingness, the world must have the ability to respond. This implies that the world has the capacity for novelty, or freedom, within itself if it is to respond to the call of God. Some say that God builds this freedom into the world; it is also possible that existence is by definition the capacity for novelty. Being itself depends upon the capacity to become. We suppose that at the level of moving from utter chaos to primal forms of order, the capacity for novelty is rudimentary. One does not leap from utter chaos to supersonic jets. But the original response of the world is of awesome importance, for that primal response sets the directions and the parameters for all successive responses. Apart from a call to order, the novelty within chaos is simply chaos. With a call to order, novelty necessarily builds upon the past, but holds within itself the capacity to go beyond the past.

The second form of novelty entailed in a call and response creation is the novelty of God. If God is the one who calls creation beyond its past, then God must be a source of novelty's direction, which is also to say that God is the source of order. If God is creator, then God is an awesome fountain of possibilities, of immense adaptability to the various responses that can or do emerge in the world. To say this, of course, is to say that God is free.

So we have a creation where God calls; creation responds. God then responds to the creation's response, and building upon it, calls yet again. Through call and response, the creation comes into being as world. It is incremental, gradual, with the creation participating in its own becoming. In the first unstructured moments, God can set down the parameters of all future becomings. As the world responds within these parameters, it increasingly participates in determining its own content. God, responding to the responses of the world, adapts the continuing creation to the creaturely responses. In the process, the possibilities emerge of the world growing to deeper levels of complexity. In the beginning, out of chaos, the bare structures in and through which order can emerge come into being. As that order actualizes itself within the creative parameters, the world moves from the simplicity of the structures themselves to the complexity of structures actualized in an increasing variety of ways. Initially, chaos makes simple creation possible, through which forms of order emerge. But with the emergence of forms of order, these forms themselves contribute to what is next possible.

Think of it like this. God calls a rudimentary world into being out of chaos. At this point, God works with an unresisting chaos to lay down structures for order: an electromagnetic field, a weak force, a strong force, gravity. But once these forces are operative, the next elements of creation are called to conform not only to God's call, but also to the parameters of these four forces. Prior to the forces' existence, a "call and response" God could bring just about any forces at all into existence, given the nonresistance of chaos. But once God calls these four forces into existence, all following stages of existence must take this first stage also into account. Creation is a covenant between God *and* the world.

Creation Through Diversity

But if God creates slowly, patiently, ever drawing the world beyond its past achievements toward deeper and richer modes of being, diversity begins to be built into creation. God's creative calls take place in light of the cumulative context of the world. But this context is the world's own responsiveness, which is then taken into account in the next call. Successive responses introduce more and more novelty into the world, which is taken into account in the next creative moment. Creation through call and response takes creatureliness into covenant. God's calling guidance is adapted to the situations of the creatures. But in order to *be* guidance, God's call also reflects the faithfulness of divine love.

If creaturely response is so integral to the Creator's call, then there is simply no way there could even be a world without great diversity. For it is one thing to speak about creation in vast unities: light, heavenly bodies, water, earth, vegetation, animals, humans. But in actuality, each of these unities bespeaks a conglomeration of mind-boggling diversities. At what level does God work? Does God work at the abstract unity of "species," or in the concrete becoming of trillions upon trillions of celluar events that are themselves composed of even smaller events? Must it not be the case that God works with the tiniest particles in bringing the larger unities into existence?

But if novelty exists within all these tiny particles, and if each responds to the call of God in light of its immediate past as well as in light of God's call, and if God responds to each individual response rather than to the conglomerate as a whole, wouldn't we expect the resultant creation to be teeming with diversity? And wouldn't this diversity be itself the result of the call of God?

Creation, Freedom, and Community

Let us leap over this discussion of a rudimentary evolutionary world to the case in point: diversity within the human community. Let us suppose that the call and response God of creation, of covenant, is just as much a call and response creator of humans as of rocks, water, and plants. So far as we know, humans are the most complex life form on this planet. Our capacity for language and for extending our senses and abilities through tools have greatly increased the pace whereby novelty yields ever new forms of existence on our planet. Our capacity for novelty is such that it deserves the name of freedom. This freedom, like all novelty, is in one sense bound by its various structured pasts, but contains an increased capacity to transcend that past relative to other forms of earthly existence.

Suppose, in this call and response creation, that God has called such beings as ourselves into existence. We are no surprise to God. From our vantage point in evolutionary time, we can look backward and see all the tiny steps that led to the possibility of our species. The path is not straight; it is more like a tree with branches and shoots moving in various directions, with "the trunk" pushing toward what we like to call its topmost realization, ourselves. Perhaps, we muse, God pulled that tree to just this growth, having us in mind all along. On the contrary, perhaps we just "grew," becoming possible on the basis of the multifarious responses of the teemingly creative relationship between God and the world. In either case, we are here as the result of God's call and the world's response—only now we personalize that world, and say that we exist as a result of God's call and *our* response. We participate in our own creation.

Because we are a new level of complexity, we say that we are "evolution become conscious of itself." We have the awesome power not simply of responding to our past, but of doing so with awareness. And that awareness itself increases our power of transcending the past, of moving in ways that reorganize the past in terms of its meaning. To deal thus with the past is in some sense to control the past, to use the past, and to transcend it in the direction of greater novelty. The role of freedom is to increase the power of the future.

But now move back to my earlier discussion of diversity in this call and response creation. If we must imagine God working at the deepest cellular level of things, why would it be different with us? If dealing minutely with creation yields particularized responses to the individualized responses of innumerable particles of existence, then we must expect this in the human world as well. After all, the Christian tradition proclaims through its doxologies, "as it was in the beginning, is now, and ever shall be" concerning the work of God with the world. Presumably God is not a chaotic creator who creates through this method here but that method there; presumably God is creator in a uniform sense.

Given the increased capacity for freedom in the human species, must we not suppose that God's response takes that freedom into account? Now turn to the Hebrew biblical texts and notice how text after text bespeaks God's call to the world as both imperative and plea! "Now the LORD said to Abram, "Go forth from your country . . . And I will make you a great nation" (Gen. 12:1, 2). The second event depends upon Abram's free response to the first. Again: "When the LORD saw that he turned aside to look, God called to him from the midst of the bush and said, 'Moses, Moses!' " (Exod. 3:4). The Lord's call and commission follow upon Moses actually turning aside to look—and then upon his obedience to the call, which is free, not forced. Again: "Then the LORD came and stood and called as at other times, "Samuel! Samuel!' And Samuel said, 'Speak, for Your servant is listening' " (1 Sam. 3:10). The oracle is given only when Samuel becomes attentive. But it is not only these few texts that indicate a God who waits for human response. The prophets emphasize the covenantal relation between God and Israel, and the sense in which God responds to Israel's actions. And is not the entire New Testament gospel a call to respond? God's continuous calls to us are adapted to our responsiveness.

But would this not be so throughout the human world? If God is continuously creator of the whole world, then God is as involved in one culture as in another. Surely God is not just a tribal deity! But the type of response God gives within any culture depends upon the type of response that those within the culture have given to God's call.

Now just here the exclusivist Christian might cry, "Gotcha! You see, everyone's response but ours is wrong!" But the texts do not support this. No matter what response the people give, God's response incorporates their reality into the next possibility, and the next possibility is always toward their good.

The impact of this is that God uses the past, whether favorable or unfavorable, to call people individually and as a whole toward greater care in and for the community. Rituals and stories such as the Genesis story become ways of organizing the teeming events of the past into an ordering structure from which and within which care of the community takes place. Religion is the binding together and bonding together of peoples into community, woven together by the sense of what is sacred. Is this not consistent with God's method of creation through call and response? Religions evolve creatively as God continuously uses the named and unnamed past to call people toward futures now possible for them.

Religions As Call and Response

In many New Testament texts scholars point out a convergence of Greek and Jewish influence, with the Jewish care for justice and Greek metaphysics coming together to create a new form of religion. Is not God's call in this? If we look at the Christian phenomenon in light of a "call and response" God, can we not consider that through the Jew Jesus, God introduced a new possibility for communal life within the gentile world? The convergence of two pasts, Jewish and gentile, created a form of religion different from either Judaism or the Greco-Roman world alone. New possibilities for communal well-being emerged, and over time new rituals and new stories developed to support the new forms of community. But God the creator is as involved in this as in the continuing evolution of Judaism itself. The faithfulness of God and the peculiarities of human diversity will ensure both difference and similarity between the two religions. But both are of God, reflecting the call and response dynamic of creation.

Shouldn't we extend the creative dynamic between God and the world to all people? Surely we would not think that God was totally unaware of those persons now called the Aborigines of Australia until England happened to notice that continent! And if God worked faithfully in a call and response way to those long-ago Jews, Greeks, and Romans, why would God be less faithful with the Aborigines? God called and still calls them to forms of community that mediate well-being, even though those forms of community are quite different from the structures that emerged in ancient Palestine or in the Greco-Roman world. Rituals and stories would emerge reflecting the novelties for community made possible within the Australian eco/human context. If God is God, then God is as surely creatively involved in the evolution of Aborigine culture as in Jewish and Christian culture.

Where shall it stop? Did God ignore the people of China, India, or Africa? Were communities of well-being incidental in those contexts, and only important in Jewish or Christian contexts? If God works through call and response, and if human freedom introduces variety into the response, then shouldn't we expect to find different stories, rituals, orders of social structure, and senses of the sacred, but all tending toward creating the good within human forms of community?

In short, a call and response theology of creation requires diversity not only in the environmental world, but also, given the increase of freedom and the consequent creation of culture, it requires diversity in the religious world as well. If God is involved in the forms of religion we call Judaism and Christianity, then God is involved in all forms of religion.

Differing Senses of the Sacred?

The caveat, I know, is that none of the religions mean the same thing in the naming of "God." Indeed, many forms of Buddhism decry the very notion of God, claiming that it introduces a dualism that belies the nature of things. But *must* God lead all religions to name exactly the same reality when they name God? Do we absolutely demand that God always act with others exactly as God acts with us? Can God have no other stories, no other relationships, no other loves? Or is it just possible that the God who interacts with a world of diversely emerging cultures devises diverse ways whereby those cultures shall become community? Each of us, peeking over the other's religious fence, might espy aspects that look something like what we ourselves have learned of God, and our temptation then is to shout, "Aha! Yes! Because that religion is like mine, I can accept that God has been at work in it!" But we have no way of knowing that in all the differences of that emergent culture, there might be ways that are quite foreign to us that might also be manifestations of God. We have criteria to judge that which is of God in our own religion, but we do not know if these criteria are applicable in other religions. And so we should stop peering over the fence and muttering to ourselves, in favor of forthright conversation with the other.

I am not developing an argument for religious diversity that commands assent from all people. I know too well that it won't command assent from all Christian people. Regardless of my dissidents, I am arguing that a Christian theology of creation, built on call and response, demands not only that there be diversity in the world of nature, but that there be diversity in cultures and religions as well. This diversity is itself the work of God in creative response to people in their various contexts in the world.

Dialogue

On this basis, I suggest it is time for Christians to cease viewing persons from other religions as candidates for conversion. Rather, they are potential partners for conversation. Friendship, not competition, should be our goal. Friends talk with each other, argue with each other, even critique each other, but the underlying friendship means that respect and caring underlie all forms of conversation. To disagree with the other is not to disparage the other, but to engage each other at the depth levels of who we are. In such dialogue, we have much to learn not only about the other, but about ourselves, and about the God we love and serve. It may even be that just as we delight in the differences represented in personal friendships, we shall begin to delight in the creative differences represented in interreligious friendships.

God is creator, ever creating. Let us honor God in honoring the works of creation. Let us delight in the manyness of things and the manyness of people.

Questions for Reflection and Discussion

- Why do you think "creation out of nothing" was such an important Christian doctrine? Does God's "Godness" depend upon there once having been nothing except God? Why or why not?

- If God's call always comes at the most fundamental level of our existence, then it would not usually be consciously perceived—we'd experience it at preconscious levels. At our conscious level, it might usually be felt as impulse, or intuition. How, then, do you suppose we discern God's call as *God's* call? Have you ever experienced what you name as God's call? What led you to think it was from God?

- If God's call depends upon our prior responses, always taking those responses into account, wouldn't God's "plans" for earthly existence always be conditional? Wouldn't God's plans for us also emerge? But this would mean that God doesn't exactly control the future of us and our planet. It depends partially on us. Does this accord with our experience? What does this say about human responsibility?

- Is it possible in this world for the varying religions to represent the various calls of God to various people in their own contexts?

How silently, how silently, the wondrous gift is given; so God imparts to human hearts the blessings of his heaven.

No ear may hear his coming, but in this world of sin,

where meek souls will receive him, still the dear Christ enters in.

—"O Little Town of Bethlehem"

We look at it and do not see it;

  Its name is The Invisible.

We listen to it and do not hear it;

  Its name is The Inaudible.

We touch it and do not find it;

  Its name is The Subtle (formless).

These three cannot be further inquired into,

And hence merge into one.

—*Tao-Te Ching* 14[1]

CHAPTER THREE

RADICAL INCARNATION

In this chapter we tackle the issue of truth. After all, we have the Johannine text, "I am the way, and the truth, and the life; no one comes to the Father but through Me" (14:6). I can almost hear the objection: "Well, Marjorie, it may well be the case that God is at work throughout creation, but if God takes human response into consideration, then some responses just cut out all possibility of access to the Truth! And truths cannot be contradictory. When religious systems speak differently about the truth, only one of those systems can be correct, right? And Christianity has the witness of Jesus that he is the truth, and consequently the way to salvation. There can only be one true religion, and it is Christianity, thank you very much."

But I modestly suggest to my objector that there is another way to look at it. I shall argue first that the issue of religious truth is often bound up with the way we abstract information from our experience in order to explain and, to some extent, control experience. What we name as "truth" ranges from the simple to the complex, and often the more complex a thing or situation is, the more it reflects aspects about ourselves as well as that about which we speak.

Next, I consider the text raised by my supposed debater in light of the issue of incarnation. The theology of creation developed in chapter 1 allows the further step of suggesting that incarnation is not only possible, but that it is radically the way God works in the world. Because of this, God not only calls all religions into existence, but is present within all religions. God is radically incarnate, whether explicitly in Christianity, or implicitly in other religions.

Finally, I suggest that the nature of religious language, plus the radical nature of incarnation, generates multiple truths. In a deep sense, all religions can be true in their descriptions of ultimate reality, even when these descriptions disagree.

Truth As the Way Things Are?

In earlier times, it was thought that the way we think about things directly corresponds with the way things are in the world, whether that be the world around us, the world within us, or the world of a spiritual universe that transcends our physical senses. Truth was a one-dimensional thing, reflecting conditions as they are. But this theory began to break down, particularly in the influential philosophy of Immanuel Kant. He argued that we only know the world as it appears to us, and that this appearance is affected by structures internal to the human brain. Thus we do not know a thing as it exists in itself, but only as it appears to us after its perception has been "filtered" through human consciousness. We know appearance, not reality. Our language about reality reflects as much about ourselves and our structures of "knowing" as it does about that which is beyond us. Whether or not Kant was right in all respects, today we know that our perspective influences our perception of things and issues. We are so immersed in our own perspectives that it is not always easy for us to see just how they add or detract from the things and issues we perceive and consider.

This is not particularly a problem in our everyday lives. If I say that there are flowers in my garden, I don't expect a response of "But that's just your perspective!" There either are or are not flowers in my garden, and all it takes is a trip to the garden to find out, one way or the other. Perspective is operative, but more at the emotional level: I might find much delight in the flowers in my garden, but to someone who may never see my garden, the fact that I am growing flowers may be neither here nor there!

But what about the less verifiable world of religious assertions? Is that the same as saying "I have flowers in my garden"? We admit that it is not when we declare the importance of faith when it comes to religious truth. Faith is required because we cannot verify religious truth in the same way that we can verify physical things, like flowers and gardens. We do not *know* that there is an absolute correspondence between what we say about God and God's relation to the world, but we *believe* that there is. The grounds of our belief are texts and traditions, communities with which we are affiliated, and our own religious experience. There is a certain circularity in this, since our interpretations of our religious experience are deeply influenced by our texts, traditions, and communities. This is obvious in the variations of belief and practice that exist among persons and communities within a single tradition, such as the differences between Baptists, Anglicans, Methodists, and Roman Catholics on issues like the sacraments. Thus to ask for the verifiability of any religious belief is much more complicated than asking whether there are flowers in my garden!

Perhaps the reasons for this complication are not so simple as our inability to check out God-and-the-universe as easily as we can check out my garden. While Immanuel Kant might have explained the difference by saying all information is changed to an indeterminable degree by the structures of our minds, the American philosopher and psychologist William James had a different way of describing why our concepts about ultimate reality are not so easily correlated with our everyday experience.

William James and the Usefulness of Abstractions

James offers an interesting perspective on the nature of concepts and truth.[2] In *A Pluralistic Universe*,[3] he argues that the power of the intellect is its ability to control reality through defining it. But definitions are not reality. They are useful abstractions from the messiness of lived experience that leave the fullness of that experience behind. The power gained over the world through these abstracted concepts is so beguiling as to lead one to think that what is *really* real is precisely those abstractions: the rational, in pure, unchanging, controllable form. The actual world, with its buzzing confusion, is of a lesser sort, and those aspects that are left out of our definitions become irrational, unreal, or irrelevant. Seeing the world through concepts, we become blind to whatever does not fit our conceptual scheme.

We further compound the problem by taking the intellect itself as the prime model of reality. Because the finite intellect can hold many concepts together within itself, we have thought that there must be an absolute intellect that embraces all concepts. This projected Absolute Reality, often named "God," becomes the substitute for the more unmanageable sensible reality of everyday life.

There is a pragmatic effect to such absolutism, for concepts do indeed allow us to make our way in the world, to manage it, to use it to our advantage. Concepts are eminently useful; we cannot do without them. But they are not substitutes for the world they describe. Indeed, James argued, concepts and the logic connecting them reduce the world to its external appearances, rendering its inwardness invisible and incomprehensible.

Abstractions and Constructs of God

As James pushes the logic of absolutism to its extreme, he shows how it yields the notion of a God totally disconnected from the world, just as language is abstracted from its roots in the world. The distant God is covered in attributes so foreign to finite existence that they render the God incommensurate with human experience.

James argued that the conceptual God of Absolutes belied the intimacy and reciprocal relation that appears to happen between God and human beings in religious experience. His earlier appeal to varieties of religious experience had highlighted aspects of religion that were usually ignored by philosophers. If we take mystical experience seriously, James said, it witnesses to a possibility within the human spirit for an openness to that which is more than the self, and yet which empowers the self: God. The witness is not to a remote deity, but to an immanent deity at the very edges of the self. Such experience suggests that the God constructed through absolutes is hardly more than an invention of the human mind, whereas the God at the edges of the self confronts us in the midst of our reality.

James and Pluralism

To apply James's description to cultural realities such as religions is in some sense primitive. Since his time we have anthropological studies, cultural studies, history of religions studies, and other studies that map out the integral relation of religions to their times and places and various influences. We know that a cross section of a religion may give it the appearance of being timeless and always-one-thing, but if we gain a more historical view, we see the sluggish river of each religion twisting and winding and changing according to its interaction with the shifting sands of its own landscape.

To look at religions from a Jamesian point of view is to suggest that each religion's vision of ultimate reality is its own cumulative abstraction of concepts from the complexities of existence in order to gain some measure of control over the difficulties of communal human living. The very power of concepts in any and every culture seduces us into making the abstractions complete, projecting a "world" of concepts. This world cannot be a mirror of reality, for concepts are not capable of grasping the whole of reality. As James notes, they must be taken as complementary to the stuff of existence, not as isolated from that stuff. When isolated, concepts become the world of creeds in one religion, or dharmas in another, or something else in yet a third. It is as if concepts on the first order are their simple abstraction from the stuff of experience, but on the second order, they are totally divested of their source in experience, gaining the power of clarity and distinctness. As they create a totally conceptualized realm, they leave off the messiness from which they came and shine in isolated splendor in a purer form. They develop their own internal forms of logic and coherence.[4] Their pragmatic usefulness is the organization of human beings into forms of community that themselves foster human survival, growth, and meaning, particularly with what is regarded as sacred.

If we force our conceptual systems back to their roots, back to the stuff from which they are abstracted—not to their loss, but to their fuller connection—then we do indeed see that our conceptual systems are relative to the contexts from which they are continuously abstracted. Their edges are not so clear as one supposes, for the stuff they poorly represent is not clear. To the contrary, the things and events of which they speak penetrate, influence, and change one another. And the concepts, if they are to be true, must also partake of change, of flow. Indeed, the static nature of concepts is more like a useful fiction than a real representation of existence, and the pure and changeless world that they have the power to create is itself the ultimate illusion. If we can allow a kind of fluidity into our concepts and our conceptual systems, keeping them grounded, we can perhaps increase their pragmatic usefulness in ordering life.

Multiple Truths?

To compare faith systems in order to determine which one is "true," then, is a most complex and perhaps impossible task. If we compare the systems only at their intellectual levels, we will find that they are necessarily incommensurate with one another. Each is the result of the particular religious culture's abstractions from its experience. The truth of each is the faith system *plus* its cultural environment, which itself spans centuries of time. The conceptual faith system reflects this time span, which is to say that there is a continuous interaction between the religious culture and its way of expressing its beliefs. The faith, including its conceptual and experiential base, is a living thing embodied in a community that continuously responds to changes in its environment. To compare faiths, then, one must compare not just the conceptual portion, but the living experience of the whole. To then ask, "Is it true?" is almost tautologous. Of course it is true! It is descriptive of the way a whole community has interpreted itself through time! "But does it correspond with the way things *really* are?" And again, the answer is ambiguous. It is the way things really are in that community. To abstract its concepts and measure them against other concepts is to miss the fullness of what that faith is about.

In this sense, then, there are multiple religious truths simply because there are multiple religious communities. It does not mean that there is not some state of affairs apart from the religious descriptions. But it does mean that the state of affairs is apparently compatible with many ways of creating communities, even though many of those communities see themselves as the only or at least the best way of describing that state of affairs. Pluralism appears to be built into the system. We see it within the complex trajectories of each religion, as well as among the religions.

Notice the movement of pluralism within Christianity itself. A Christian vision of reality, moving from a European context into an American context, begins to reflect the peculiarities emergent from the émigrés' interaction with their environment, their history, their particularities. Likewise, a Christian vision of reality moving from its American context into a Korean context begins to reflect shamanistic and Confucian sensitivities. R. S. Sugirtharajah's book, *Asian Faces of Jesus*,[5] is a dramatic illustration of the transmutation of Christology when it is developed from Asian rather than European or American culture. It's something akin to taking a single pattern to make many dresses, some of homespun cotton, others of African prints, others of Asian silk. Each dress requires variations appropriate to the material. While the pattern is the same, the resulting dresses are quite different.

And the same is true when other religions, such as Buddhism, take root on Christian soil. In my early studies of Buddhism I read the works of Alan Watts, a Christian-become-Buddhist, and was struck by how similar the patterns of Buddhism were to evangelical forms of Christianity. But when I read the *Lotus Sutra,* and Japanese interpreters of Buddhism, Buddhism was no longer quite so like evangelical Christianity. Concepts and contexts are intertwined; there is no pure conceptual realm save in our imaginations.

An Incarnational World

So, then, does my dialogue with James simply reinforce a religious pluralism that leads us down the relativistic pathway? Not quite. And now I ask you to hold this discussion of abstractions and creeds in abeyance, and return to the conceptuality I acquainted you with earlier, that of process thought. While abstractions are not exact mirrors of reality, they nonetheless give intimations of reality, since they are rooted in the complexities of experience.

Charles Sanders Peirce thought of it this way: The rationality of which we are so proud is no stranger in this world. To the contrary, it is part and parcel of a world that is in itself rational. By this he meant—and I mean—that the world in which we live yields rational insight. There are relationships between things, there is a uniformity to the processes we experience and observe, there are mathematical equivalents to the way processes work. The rationality that we experience within ourselves is continuous with the rest of this earth, this solar system, this galaxy, this universe. We are not aliens plunked down on a mysterious planet, we have ourselves emerged from the stuff of this planet, and so, like the planet, we ourselves are rational. In a sense, we are rationality thinking itself—or, in a phrase more common, evolution become conscious of itself.

But the world is more than rationality. The world is thick with experience. Rationality attempts to express that which is more than it can express, and hence rationality itself can follow diverse forms. This is what abstraction means. And it is why poetry, music, and painting, with their intimations and nuances, have the power to speak with a fullness surpassing our philosophies. There is always more than we can say. Language speaks inexhaustibly about that which is, finally, inexhaustible.

In my previous chapter I argued that God is operative *in* the world; not over the world, not on the world, but *in* the world. God works, I suggested, through call and response. God calls, and the world responds, and these calls and responses take place in as many ways as there are cells and molecules and atoms to respond to the call of God. Let's take this a step further. Metaphorically speaking, how does a cell, a molecule, an atom, *hear* the call of God? Hearing belongs to living creatures, not to the minute particles of which we are composed. How, then, do we say that God speaks in such a way that the most minute creaturely existence has the capacity to respond—or not respond—to this call?

And here is where the notion of incarnation becomes radical. Within the Christian tradition we have long held that in Jesus of Nazareth we see the nature of God revealed for us. We have explained this by saying that God is incarnate in Jesus, so that in dealing with him, we deal as well with God. Clearly, this creates problems for most other traditions, because it seems to privilege Christianity over the others. But stay for a while with the insight. Alfred North Whitehead suggests that to exist is to feel a past, along with its impact upon one's own possibilities for becoming. To exist is also to feel a future, as that which one truly might become. In between this past and this future is the struggle of the present, coming into its promised land through the influence of the past and the pull of the future.

It is easy to account for the source of the past on the becoming moment, for every new existent reality is thrown into a preexistent state of affairs that exerts an influence toward conformity. That which has been calls for its own repetition in the becoming present. But what is the source of the future? It does not yet exist, how does it exercise a pull toward itself?

It's not the case that we can account for all possibilities from the past alone, for there are too many cases where genuine novelty emerges. To walk into the Grand Canyon is to experience this: One literally traces a move from complexity in the fossilized life-forms near the Canyon's surface to simplicity in the earlier levels of those Canyon walls, and many gradations in between. History is literally embedded in stone. At the bottom of the Canyon the shell forms are simple; at the upper reaches of the Canyon the shell forms are complex. The simple did not contain the complex; when complex shell life emerged it was a leap beyond its past to a new form of existence. It moved into a future that transcended all achievements of its past. Presumably shell life has no consciousness as we know it, such that it could imagine possibilities that go beyond its past. What accounts for the pull toward its future? How did it "know" throughout its successive generations that it could evolve into new forms?

Play with the notion that the simple and the complex answer is God. God grounds the possibilities of the world, and the call of God to each moment is a call toward what, given its past, it may yet become. But that call comes as an influence, even as the past comes as an influence. God's call is an influence toward whatever form of becoming suits this time, this place, this emergent piece of reality. In responding to the call, the new bit of existence takes that influence into itself, either negating it or adjusting it to its past, adapting it, or conforming to it, depending upon its own determination. That which God offers as future is taken into the becoming moment.

But if God offers a possibility drawn from the resources of the divine life, then one could imagine that by receiving the influence of God, the reality that then embodies that influence is to one degree or other an incarnation of God in the world. Incarnation, then, would be radical, not limited to a single person, but possible throughout existence. To the same degree that the becoming reality takes the influence of God into its own becoming, the reality is a reflection of God for this time, place, or circumstance.

Will it be a universal reflection of God? Of course not. It is a timely reflection. Will it be a full reflection of God? Of course not. It is an adaptation of the purposes of God as suitable to this time, this place. But it is nonetheless an incarnation of God in the world.

Incarnation and Culture

Now, then, let me take you back to the complexities of incarnation in the human world, and weave the discussion into the nature of abstractions. In my previous chapter I suggested that God is involved in the development of culture. How? According to this conceptuality, God is incarnate in every culture through the dynamism just presented.

Each culture is a story, built up through many centuries, through which humans have developed and honed the capacity to exist meaningfully together in community. Communal existence is essential for our survival. We are social creatures with many needs, requiring one another for the fulfillment of those needs and thus for our continuation in time. Our bonding together is our survival. Cultures are the stories of our survival through generations.

Our need for bonding with one another is matched by our need for bonding with the environing earth. We need the sustaining food, air, and water that earth provides. Hence, culture is not only the story of our bonding with others like ourselves, it is also the story of the ways we have bonded with this earth.

Each culture develops its own trajectory. Language is the unique tool through which we develop that trajectory, sometimes through story either as ritual or history or both, sometimes as poetry, sometimes as abstract formulations of meaning. The function of stories, rituals, history, poetry, and formulations of meaning is to structure the ongoing community in ways that conform to the past and also transform the past. Conformation to the past is conformation to the tried-and-true; it is the reception and guardianship of a particular heritage, which is a particular way of ensuring that the community shall continue. Transformation occurs because the dynamism of life itself is such that the past can never be simply repeated. The persons and their relationships are different, even while similar to those preceding. While the past is repeated, it necessarily is repeated with a difference. Some differences enhance the community and become incorporated into the ongoing story, turning it into history. Some differences endanger the received way of being, and are either refuted or adapted. Whether they are refuted or adapted, they affect the ongoing tradition, which is necessarily changed by encounter with its challenge. In a deep sense, traditions are created in and through their transformations, wherein story becomes history.

God in Culture

I have posited that God interacts with the creation of human culture by calling cultures toward increasingly complex forms of community. Response to God's call is the incorporation of God's influence into the tradition's becoming; it is the incarnation of God relative to that time, that place, that possibility for community.

Earlier I argued that language is our most amazing tool for organizing our experience. Through language we make meaning, and the meanings we make become the goals that draw us toward fulfillment in one way or another. Language is an abstraction from our immersion in experience, giving us some measure of control over experience. The control takes many forms. It may be formulation of rules for communal life, or it may be visionary, drawing us toward that which we name as our highest good. But whether rule-oriented or vision-oriented, language guides creation of ourselves within our communities. In a sense, language is always taking place in the middle of a story, for our languages abstract from the messiness of given experience and so guide our interpretations and organizations of new experience.

But if God is involved in our experience by influencing us toward more complex forms of community, and if God's influence is incarnational, then our languages that abstract from experience are also abstractions from our various experiences of God. And if God is pervasively active throughout the world, such that God is God of the universe and all that is in it, then there are no linguistic systems that do not, to some degree, reflect God's work within the culture in question.

But you will remember my objector—indeed, you yourself might be that objector—protesting that we can't name all cultural projections as reflections of God, because the cultural perceptions are quite different! How can God be all those things? How can God be yin and yang, or the Tao; how can God be a compassionate Buddha; how can God be an Allah, a Jehovah, a Trinity, and a Brahma-Shiva-Vishnu all at once? Preposterous!

But think a minute. The supposition is that God calls us to modes of more complex and richer ways of surviving, living, caring, and making meaning. The goal of God's call within each culture is toward richness and inclusiveness of community (I shall argue this in my next chapter). The abstractions that make their ways into metaphysical speculations are drawn from the guidance toward community, and are ways of expressing that which has enabled the community's becoming in a particular context over a particular period of human time. And if God has been in that call toward community, won't God, reflected in that community, be apparent in the abstract visions?

God of Light

We have an interesting phenomenon in our world that might get us over the conflicts and contradictions within the various faith communities. Think of the wonders of light. A system was devised by which to measure light, and when it was applied, light was broken down into particles. The fundamental nature of light, then, was discovered to be particulate! But alas, when another system was used to measure light, light was found to be waves! And this, of course, indicated that the fundamental nature of light is that of a continuous wave. We know that according to the law of noncontradiction, something cannot be both a particle and a wave. It is either one or the other. But both forms of measurement are accurate. So we must finally admit that light, when measured one way, is a wave, but when measured another way, is a particle. It's not that the wave is a pseudolight, some fake approximation of light, with only the particle being accurate. Nor is it the reverse. Rather, light seems to be malleable. It has the power to become different things, depending upon its interaction with the measuring device. It is not a question of true or false, it is a question of this or that, depending on how it is measured.

If light can turn out to be two quite different things, with these differing things not canceling the other out, why do we think that God must be simpler than light? Have we not said in our various ways that God is light? "God is light," says one religious text, "and in Him there is no darkness at all" (1 John 1:5). "In Your light we see light" (Ps. 36:9), we say, and "The LORD is my light and my salvation; Whom shall I fear?" (Ps. 27:1). Perhaps God measured in one culture, through that which God has truly given in and through God's incarnational influence within that culture, becomes nonpersonal. Perhaps that which we in our culture call God could be, through Buddhist measurement, no God at all! And even though this nondualistic "no God" is quite different from what a Christian or a Jew or a Muslim might call God, perhaps this is because we use a different measuring device. Perhaps theistic cultures, in which God is also incarnate, measure that pervasive call to our future and see, with variations, that which we name as God.

And yet there's the rub. Our ways of talking about God are abstractions from our experience. Our concepts are no more God than our concept of music is music itself. We have abstracted from that which God has truly given to each culture; we yank God from the messiness of this fulsome life, wipe off the mud of experience, and place the shined-up concept of God on an idealistic pedestal in isolated splendor, there to receive our worship. And all the while God continues to move in and through our experience. We live and move and have our being in God even as we mistake our polished concept of God for God's own self. Whitehead would call it the fallacy of misplaced concreteness.

So, God is involved in the evolutionary production of all worlds. The data of evolution to date indicate that order is an inordinately complex thing appearing to us more often as chaos, and since in this enormously complicated ordering of things there is never just one trajectory, but many trajectories, and since these trajectories can only be marked as trajectories from a backward glance—tracing the past rather than the future—then we might conclude that God deals not with one story, but with an infinite number of stories. Notions of the simplicity of God so traditional in Christian history would have spoken more realistically to the simplicity of concepts, not of reality—particularly not the reality of God.

God participates directly in the messiness of concrete stuff, and only indirectly in the conceptual order. Thus the conceptual order is not the clearest route to this God, much less the clearest reflection of this God. Traditionally, God was approached through abstractions because God so far transcended the world that only abstractions could come near to God. But in a Jamesian world, abstractions are not from the world toward God, they are from the world and away from God, for God is experienced immanently, in the world. Just as systems of religion are conceptual schemes, they are also abstractions from the experience of God in the world. Rather than pointing away from the world to a supposed still-greater purity than themselves, whether monistic or dualistic, whether called God, or the Absolute, or Ultimate Reality, or any other name, they might be better advised to point back to the world from whence they came, and there look for ultimacy.

This would mean, of course, that all religions have their root in ultimacy, albeit their conceptualizations of this must vary. Even if one states that religions are conceptual, comparing their conceptualities to determine which one is "true" misses the point. Comparing systems will reveal alternative forms of internally logical truth, but not reality. God is not to be found in conceptual systems, but in the messiness of evolutionary life. The expressions of this God, and the ultimacy thus represented, will necessarily be pluralistic.

And "No One Comes to the Father but Through Me"

At the beginning of this chapter I offered to deal with the specific Christian text attributed to Jesus, "I am the way, and the truth, and the life; no one comes to the Father but through Me." Surely we who are Christian have a long history of taking this text quite seriously, to the point of considering all humans who see things differently from ourselves as consigned to some outer darkness or worse. I hope my work of first discussing the abstractive nature of language, and second, the incarnational nature of God, casts light on this scriptural text.

A brief digression may be helpful. I have recently taught Karl Barth's *Dogmatics in Outline* to a master of divinity class. One thundering aspect of Barth's theology is the Fatherhood of God—indeed, Barth is willing to call almost anything metaphorical for God, except the name of Father: God is Father, period. In assuming or arguing this, Barth is solidly within the Christian tradition, however much we feminists might wince. In this particular Christian culture, the notion of God has been a dominantly male notion that at root is associated with fatherhood. God is called the "God and Father of our Lord Jesus Christ" (Rom. 15:6), and through Christ Christians have "our access in one Spirit to the Father" (Eph. 2:18).

I suggest to you that it is literally true that persons who come to God as father in this sense do so in and through Jesus Christ and the tradition built upon adherence to God through him. "God as Father" is an abstraction from the fullness of Christian experience. I could parallel the point by saying that no one comes to God as Allah save through Muhammad. How we name God reflects the cultural traditions through which we have been formed or transformed, and each is true. For me as a Christian, Jesus is indeed the way, the truth, and the light. Through him I know what it means to name God "Father"—not in a "God as male" sense, but in a "God as infinite caring" sense. Through Jesus, I have come to know God as father.

But I am deeply convinced that there are parallel truths. My naming of God through Jesus Christ reflects the work of God with me and the tradition in which I stand, and it truly names God. A Jewish naming of God reflects the work of God with Jews in the tradition in which they stand. We are each naming the way God has worked with us respectively. Wave and particle are both truly light, and we live in a radically incarnational world where truth itself is a many-splendored thing.

Questions for Reflection and Discussion

- If we grant that there are "multiple truths," each reflecting God's work within a particular culture, why should we follow one rather than another? Is it an "anything goes" world of religions?

- If our cultures are a part of who we are—more like a part of our bones than a part of the clothes we wear—how can there be religious conversions from one cultural form of religion to another?

- Is it really possible to cherish the truths of one's own religion and at the same time honor the truths of another?

- Can we say, along with Ernst Troeltsch, that Christianity is absolutely true—for Christians?

- Can we be comfortable with God's call to us to be Christians if we think that God calls other folks to be Buddhists, Jews, Muslims, Hindus, or some other religion? If God calls us to be Christians, shouldn't God call everybody to be Christians?

Then God said, "Let Us make man in Our image, according to Our likeness; and let them rule over the fish of the sea and over the birds of the sky and over the cattle and over all the earth, and over every creeping thing that creeps on the earth."

God created man in His own image, in the image of God He created him; male and female He created them.

—Gen. 1:26-27

To God belong the East and the West;

withersoever you turn, there is the Face of God;

God is All-embracing, All-knowing.

—The Koran (interpreted) 2.108[1]

CHAPTER FOUR

THE IMAGE OF GOD

In my creation chapter I argued for the dynamic of God in the world, suggesting that this dynamic requires an affirmation of religious pluralism. Evolution itself requires diversity and multiplicity, and this extends to cultural evolution as well as biological evolution. The chapter on radical incarnation argued first that our concepts (including our doctrines) are abstractions from experience and cannot contain the fullness of experience; second, that our concepts are therefore rooted in the cultures from which they are derived. I suggested that God is involved incarnationally in every culture, and therefore that God's leading is also reflected in each culture's various conceptual schemes. This leads to multiple forms of truth as the conceptualizations of various communal experiences.

In neither chapter was there a criterion for discerning the work of God. Are we in an "anything goes" world of religions? This, of course, would launch us into the proverbial sea of relativism that is the anathema of all religious traditions, and the particular bane of those striving to affirm religious pluralism. The religions themselves provide arguments against a world of sheer relativism, for inherent within each religion are criteria for judging that which is good. Dialogue among the religions includes, among other things, discussion of their various criteria. Within the

Christian natural theology that I am developing here, there is a hint of a Christian criterion insofar as I suggested that community formation is involved in the work of God. In these next two chapters I will further develop that criterion. The present chapter does so by continuing to draw from the Genesis text, this time in connection with interpretations of the image of God.

A Criterion for Religion

Arguing for pluralism is one thing, but arguing for a criterion by which to judge the pluralism becomes a bit more dangerous. Of course the suspicion of those from other traditions is, "There they go again! Those Christians are forever developing criteria that are little more than extensions of their own norms and values to cover us all! Christian imperialism wins again!" Recognizing the validity of this suspicion, I offer the following criterion of community formation not as a universal criterion, but as one that operates within one tradition even while it borrows from another, Judaism. A pluralistic world is not an "anything goes" world. We do not magically suspend all judgments just because we are talking with those with whom we disagree about religion. We each bring criteria to the table, and one important task is to clarify the criteria we bring. We are not adrift in a sea of relativism; we are working from our own particular measurement of the light that is given to us.

There are two aspects of a criterion involving the notion of community. The first is developed from the belief that humanity is created in the image of God, and the second, to be developed in my next chapter, is the conviction that God calls us to a manifestation of the reign of God in human community, with this reign being a world community of diverse communities, each of which lives justly. With regard to the "image of God," I will briefly summarize what this phrase has meant in the Christian tradition. I will then suggest that "image of God" is a necessarily communal term, marking the "godliness" of divine influence upon us, and therefore serving as a criterion for Christian affirmation of other religions. The worth of a criterion is fundamentally twofold. It serves for internal self-correction within the tradition from which the criterion is drawn, and it serves externally in interreligious dialogue as we learn from one another.

The Image of God in Scripture

My thesis is that religious pluralism is a positive reality, not despite the competing truth claims of the various religions, but even because of these claims. Religious pluralism is, in fact, essential to achieving some approximation of what we in Christian history have called the image of God. The phrase, "image of God," is taken, of course, from the first chapter of Genesis.

"Then God said, 'Let Us make man in Our image, according to Our likeness; and let them rule over the fish of the sea and over the birds of the sky and over the cattle and over all the earth, and over every creeping thing that creeps on the earth. God created man in His own image, in the image of God He created him; male and female He created them" (1:26-27).

These simple words have a long history of Christian interpretation. Biblically, the words do not function strongly within the Hebrew writings. "Image of God" occurs only three times, and that within the first nine books of Genesis. In addition to the text cited, we also have Genesis 5:1-3, which reiterates God's creation of humans in the likeness of God, male and female, blessing us. In Genesis 9:6 the phrase returns again in connection with the covenant with Noah. God gives us all things, including animals, for food, but this authorization to kill for the sake of life has limits. Humans are not to eat flesh "with its blood," which has implications for dietary laws. And even more important, "Whoever sheds man's blood, By man his blood shall be shed, For in the image of God [God] made man." Following this comes the reiteration of Genesis 1:28, telling Noah to be fruitful and to multiply. Aside from these verses, which scholars consider to be priestly texts originating during the Babylonian exile, the phrase "image of God" does not recur in the Hebrew scriptures.

Scholars tell us that the phrase may have Egyptian and Mesopotamian origins. In Egypt, an image of God was considered to be the place where deity manifested itself. The implication of the Genesis text, then, would be that while God is creator of all that exists, God is peculiarly manifested within the human community. From Mesopotamia, the phrase is associated with royalty as the peculiar place where God is manifest. The Genesis text democratizes the phrase, making it apply to humanity per se, and not to a representative portion of humanity.

Because the phrase "image of God" is immediately followed by language of stewardship over the earth and its creatures, there are implications that to be in the image of God is to mirror the activity of God relative to the rest of creation. The foregoing text indicates that God is an ordering God, a creative God, a God who calls each thing into its own becoming toward its good. Furthermore, the good of each thing relates to the good of other things, for in the text, each thing prepares the way for the next thing, and God pronounces all of it good. Humans, then, if they are in God's image, would also be responsible for nurturing the good of the earth in creative ways. This indicates that one aspect of the divine image is the responsibility to care for the earth in its particulars and also in its wholeness.

But what of the use of "image of God" in the New Testament? While the phrase is not picked up and developed throughout Hebrew scripture, it surely is in Christian scripture and tradition. The first reason, of course, is the use made of the phrase in the epistles of the New Testament, most notably Colossians 1:15-16: "[Christ] is the image of the invisible God, the firstborn of all creation. For by Him all things were created, *both* in the heavens and on earth." The image of God that denoted all humanity in Genesis is now focused on Jesus as the Christ—a narrowing that became momentous in the Christian tradition.

The Image of God in the Tradition

The Christian tradition conflated the first and second chapters of Genesis, reading Adam as created in the image of God. Because Adam sinned, so the story goes, the image was either distorted or in some sense destroyed, a calamity that was passed down to all of Adam's descendants. Christ, then, became the second Adam, and through obedience restored the image of God for humanity. To be united with Christ is therefore, at the same time, to be restored in some sense to the image of God.

Within the general framework of this basic story, theologians disagreed as to what, precisely, "image of God" is. Irenaeus, theologian of the second century, distinguished between "image" and "likeness," holding that to be made in the image of God was to have the capacity to be like God. He understood this capacity to be damaged by Adam's fall, but restored in Christ. The purpose of the church, then, is to foster us in the likeness of Christ, who is the very likeness of God. This "likeness" is the capacity to behold God. And this, in turn, is Christian maturity. Since God is good, just, and wise, to attain the likeness of God is to become good, just, and wise. To this end Irenaeus understood our lives on earth were to be spent in a "schoolhouse," developing our capacity to behold God, with the "graduation ceremony" death itself. At death we move on to participate in God's immortality, and thus gain the final achievement of the full likeness of God for which we were created.

But Augustine, writing in the fourth and fifth centuries, is the major theologian of the Christian church. Augustine comes at the notion of the "image and likeness of God" not simply through his theological predecessors, such as Irenaeus, but also through the profound influence of the third-century philosopher Plotinus. In the works of Plotinus, "image" is highly significant, for all things are the image of that from which they proceed. The procession of creation is a series of successive movements away from the primal principle, the One. The One generates the Nous, or divine Mind, which is an image of the One, but inferior to the One insofar as Mind contains duality within itself. However, as Mind contemplates the One, its image of the One intensifies, so that like the One, it generates that which is other to itself. The Mind generates the World Soul. Soul, which is now twice removed from the first principle of the One, contains not simply duality, but multiplicity. It contemplates not the One, but the Mind from which it has immediately proceeded. In contemplating Mind, Soul—like Mind and like the One before it—also generates otherness; in this case, the world in all its physical and mental particularities. The metaphysical system is complex, but the point is that for Plotinus "image" implies the contemplation of that from which one has been generated. In and through contemplation, the image is intensified, producing whatever likeness is possible. But the likeness will always be less than that from which it proceeds.

Augustine, student of the works of Plotinus, carries this thought with him as he builds his own interpretation of the Genesis text, "image of God." In *The City of God* he writes, "Let us gaze at God's image in ourselves, and, 'returning to ourselves' like the younger son in the gospel story, let us rise up and go back to God from whom we have departed in our sinning."[2] And what is this image, precisely? It is the mind contained within the soul, with the ability to perceive itself as a distant parallel to God as Trinity. God is a Trinity of eternity, truth, and love, also expressed by Augustine as God's being, God's knowledge of God's being, and God's delight in being. The human mind knows that it exists and is glad of its existence and knowledge. This is its own dim echo of the Trinity. Contemplation of God draws the soul toward love of God, which in turn intensifies the image of God within the soul.

Augustine, like Irenaeus, considers the image compromised by sin, and like Irenaeus he considers the image of God to be restored in Christ. In the same way that we are joined to Christ, the image is restored in the Christian as well. Like Irenaeus, Augustine emphasized the eschatological element of immortality, but he has gone beyond Irenaeus in his specific equation of the image of God with reason. The force of this is to increase the individualization of the image of God as that which takes place in the individual soul of individual human beings, even though this individualistic image is specifically patterned after God as triune.

This individualism is mitigated somewhat by Augustine's expansion of God as love in a Trinitarian fashion. Love, to be love, demands both a lover and a beloved. God as Father is the lover, and God as Son is the beloved. God as Spirit is the love that unites Father and Son. Love, then, can also be the image of God, and to an extent this also functions for Augustine, since those who belong to the City of God are defined by their love of God, and their consequent love of the world in and through God. This could have provided a more communal dimension to Augustine's image of God, but instead, reason was given the dominant role as that within the human being that is a reflection of God.

Augustine's notions deeply influenced the ongoing tradition; you can hear them echoed in eleventh-century Anselm in the following quotation: "For if the mind itself alone among all created beings is capable of remembering and conceiving of and loving itself, I do not see why it should be denied that it is the true image of that being which, through its memory and intelligence and love, is united in an ineffable Trinity."[3]

Thomas Aquinas is the great reshaper of Augustine. He, even more than Augustine, emphasized the intellectual nature of the image of God. God is pure intellect. Our own intellectual capacities are in no way in the same category as the divine, but insofar as our intellects exercise the act of knowing, we are analogically in the image of God. This is the highest spiritual power of the soul. Like Augustine, Aquinas expressed this power in a way that mirrored the trinitarian nature of God. The divine life is the coincidence of memory, intellect, and will. Our own intellectual nature exercises two modes of being, that of memory and that of will. Thus for Thomas, as for Augustine, for the soul to be intellectual is for the soul to be in the image of the trinitarian God. In this perfection, the image of God in Adam was an original righteousness that was full conformity to God's will.[4]

Thomas made a further tripartite distinction of the image of God corresponding to the states of human existence, understood to be nature, grace, and glory. By nature, we are created with intellectual capacities, and so we are in the image of God. This includes the potential to know and love God, for to be human is to be created toward God as our end. But nature alone must be supplemented by the grace of God if we are to attain our goal of blessedness, so the natural intellectual image of God is re-created by grace toward conformity of the human intellect with the vision of God to whatever degree is possible in our finite condition. Finally, of course, this life alone is not sufficient to the fullness of God. The full perfection of the divine image awaits the heavenly state of glory, when the soul is in the immediate presence of God, and is at last capable of full conformity to the beatific vision. This final perfection is perfect conformity to God in perfect knowledge and perfect love. Thus for Thomas there is a tripartite analysis of the image itself in this life as intellect with memory and will, and a progressive analysis that is also tripartite, moving from creation to re-creation to assimilation.

Have we come a long way from the Genesis text? Bear with me a little longer as I briefly summarize a Reformation version of the image of God, a Wesleyan view, and then inject several twentieth-century views.

Like Thomas, Martin Luther speaks of the light of nature, the light of grace, and the light of glory. In his commentary on the book of Genesis, Luther writes that the image of God sets humans far above any other form of creation, and hence the image of God can have nothing to do with that which humans share with other creatures. Thus, Luther considers the image of God to refer to an immortal aspect of humanity, and he hesitantly follows the teaching of the tradition by associating the image with memory, intellect, and will. The hesitancy is because Luther considers this image almost beyond our present imagination, given the devastation that sin has wrought in the human soul. While we do indeed have memory, intellect, and will, they are so depraved as barely to indicate to us anything at all about God. Something far more "distinguished and excellent" than what we presently call memory, intellect, and will must be signified by the image of God. And Luther then gives reign to his imagination by suggesting that every power belonging to Adam must have been of the very purest kind, and this absolute purity of being constituted the divine image. He sums up his understanding of the image in this way: "Adam had it in his being that he not only knew God and believed that He was good, but that he also lived a life that was wholly godly; that is, he was without the fear of death or of any other danger, and was content with God's favor. . . . It was as though [God] said, 'Adam and Eve, now you are living without fear; death you have not experienced, nor have you seen it. This is my image, by which you are living, just as God lives. But if you sin, you will lose this image, and you will die.' "5 For Luther, then, Adam was in the image of God in that he was without fear, in supreme bliss, and with intuitive knowledge of all things created. Clearly, original sin was calamitous, bringing an abrupt end to such goodness, and now we have but a bare intimation of what the full image as possessed by Adam could have been.

But of course Luther does not leave us in this lamentable state, for the purpose of Christ is to restore us to the image for which we were created. Christ is himself the express image of God, and in our union with Christ through baptism, we participate once more in God's image by faith. Like Thomas, Luther claims that grace takes us but so far; we must await glory for our full conformity to the image of God. Now we have it by faith; in glory, we shall have it by sight.

Notice the progression of this history. The image of God is understood in a trinitarian way, but not in a communal way. Augustine, Thomas, and Luther are giants in the theological tradition, brilliantly receiving the tradition and transforming it in ways that indelibly shape the future of all Christian theology. While each relates the image of God to the Christian confession that God is triune, the interpretation of the image has to do with each human soul. The individual as such is in the image of God, with the further stipulation that the image is indelibly connected with the individual's capacity to reason.

A brief respite from this overemphasis on reason comes from John Wesley. In his small book, *A Plain Account of Christian Perfection*, the phrase "image of God" recurs like a refrain.6 Wesley, like Luther, considered that God created Adam as a perfect kind of finite being. Wesley stipulated that all of Adam's powers—intellectual, emotional, and physical—were developed fully in order to glorify God. But the glory of God, for Wesley, is not God's superior intellect, but God's love. And the image of God in *A Plain Account of Christian Perfection* is precisely a heart filled to overflowing with love toward God and toward one another.

Charles Wesley, that great theologian-in-hymnody, phrases it well in a lengthy hymn based on the motif of Jacob wrestling with the angel. The theme of the hymn is Jacob's deep desire to know the name of the angel, of God. And the hymn culminates with the awesome phrase, "thy nature and thy name is Love."7 The image of God for the Wesleys adds to the tradition, not by canceling reason as the image of God, but by expanding the image to be the fullness of human powers given to the service and glory of God in love.

Major twentieth-century theologians who retain the usefulness of the notion "image of God" do not depart in radical ways from the individualism of the tradition. Karl Barth sees the image of God as a point of contact that existed in the original creation of the human, but was destroyed through sin. Paul Tillich injects freedom into the equation, seeing reason as the essential structure of freedom. For Tillich, humans are created in the image of God in that they are created toward freedom. Reinhold Niebuhr understands the image of God to be the human capacity for self-transcendence. While each of these major twentieth-century theologians retained the individualistic notion of the image, Karl Barth introduced a somewhat communal note by heeding the "male and female" language of the Genesis 1:26 text. In *Church Dogmatics* III, *The Doctrine of Creation* 4, he built upon earlier discussions of the human as destined for covenant partnership with God. This covenant partnership with God receives a parallel expression in the individual's covenant partnership with others, notably the partnership between man and woman. But while Barth presents the image of God text in terms of human partnership, he nonetheless considers that the original image, which was direct and free communion with God, is totally lost in sin.

Construction: The Image of God and Affirmation of Pluralism

And why, you might ask, does digression into this brief history of the Christian understanding of the image of God become a basis for affirming religious pluralism? Could one not equally well take it as grounds for Christian exclusivism? After all, if the image is lost or terribly distorted in all but those who come to Christ, and if the image is associated with reason, wouldn't this imply that persons who are not Christian have little or no reason? Certainly if the aspect of reason that is lost is the ability to know God, then all except Christians are hopelessly addled religiously speaking. How can the traditional interpretation of the image of God help at all in affirming religious pluralism?

The aspect of the tradition that I find helpful is the Christian association of the image of God with the trinitarian nature of God. In differentiation from the tradition, I suggest that if the image reflects trinitarianism, then the image must be communal, not individual. A Christian understanding of the Trinity necessarily argues that the very nature of God is a depth of unity that is established in and through irreducible diversity. The image of God in us, then, if it is truly analogical (as aspects of the tradition maintain), must likewise be a kind of unity that is established in and through irreducible diversity. But this cannot be achieved by any individual alone. To the contrary, it requires communal development. For the human to be made in the image of God is for the human to exist in community that is itself created in and through irreducible diversity. While this can and does happen within Christianity itself, its ultimate expression can only be developed as Christianity extends itself in friendship to those who are irreducibly different from Christianity. In today's world religious pluralism provides a world of irreducible diversity. In the same way that Christianity opens itself to communal relations with those who are irreducibly other, Christianity is living from and toward a call to be the image of God.

Let me flesh out the details of this argument. Whether one refers to Augustine, Anselm, Aquinas, Luther, Wesley, or twentieth-century theologians, the image of God is uniformly developed in relationship to God as triune. Arguably, this is necessary for any Christian understanding of the image of God, for this tradition is unique in its confession of God as Trinity. And more than one Christian theological commentator has seized with alacrity on the plural language of God used in the Genesis text, leaping from the text to an assertion of God's triune nature.

All developments of the Trinity, whether in the East or the West, have had the challenge of maintaining the unity of God. It is not three gods who are worshiped, but one God. The simplicity and complexity of God have created tensions not always easily resolved. But however developed, Christian theologians have been unanimous in claiming that the Father is never the Son or the Spirit; the Son is never the Father or the Spirit; and the Spirit is never the Father or the Son. The unity of God is created in and through irreducible diversity. The distinctions have been described variously. As noted in Augustine and Aquinas, they are analogous to what we would call psychological categories of being, intellect, and will. Being is usually associated primarily, but not exclusively, with the Father; intellect primarily, but not exclusively, with the Son; and will primarily, but not exclusively, with the Spirit. Sometimes the distinctions have been described in terms of eternal origins, which has occasioned an astonishing amount of Christian antagonism between Eastern and Western Christianity. The Father is ungenerate; the Son is generated from the Father; and the Spirit proceeds from the Father and the Son (the infamous Filioque clause added to the Nicene Creed), or alternatively in the east, from the Father alone through the Son. In all cases, the distinctions are absolute. Any attempt to merge them either monarchically or monistically is repudiated as rank heresy.

Given these absolute distinctions, is the unity of God anything other than a groundless verbal assertion? A fundamental way of describing God's unity is through the language of "perichoretic love," which is often (not always) interpreted after the Greek words meaning "around" and "dance." The love that *is* God is an intricate and intimate dancing and weaving wherein Father, Son, and Spirit are inexhaustibly indwelling one another. This "one" is not reducible to number; it is, rather, a unitive way of being. Trinity implies that God, in being deepest unity, is so through infinite complexity.

There is one further step that becomes deeply important in considering religious pluralism. Obviously, we have a world, so something is in existence that is not God. The Christian tradition has said in various ways that the love that defines the divine nature is such that God does not choose to contain that love solely within the divine nature itself, but—in an echo of Plato's famous dictum, "the good is diffusive of itself"—chooses to create that which is other to God in order to love that other. The otherness that is within God chooses to create an otherness that is outside of God.

One value of the trinitarian tradition is that it transcends, to some extent, our tendencies to be anthropomorphic when speaking of God, simply projecting what we know as being human onto a larger screen and calling it God. And indeed, the Christian tendency to interpret trinity analogously in terms of being, intellect, and will veered in just this direction. But God is more than human, and human categories are defied in attempting any definition of God. Yet faith asserts on the basis of the Genesis text that we are made in God's image. I submit that a single individual is not sufficient to bear God's image; that the image of God is not reducible to an individual's intellect alone, nor to freedom, self-transcendence, or any individual human quality alone. If God is convincingly portrayed as a complex unity that can only be expressed through irreducible diversity, then community, rather than individuality, is required for creaturely imaging of God.

The original Genesis text bespeaks irreducible diversity in connection with the image by immediately following the naming of the image with the naming of male and female. Men are usually not women, and women are usually not men. We are irreducibly diverse, but so structured that we tend toward one another, yearn toward one another, and can experience with one another one of the deepest unions known to us. But while this can be so with male and female, it is also true in relations of partnership, friendship, or kin. In every case of human bonding a unity is created through the differences and similarities we bear to one another.

Christians might argue that the irreducible diversity aspect of the image is already mirrored in the church through the fact that persons from so many cultures throughout the world are Christians. Diversity within the church should indeed be celebrated for theological as well as existential reasons. If it takes diversity-in-unity to create God's image, then only a diverse church is responding adequately to God's call. But this alone is not enough. Within the trinitarian tradition, it is precisely because of God's inner diversity that God is love, and because of this internal love God creates that which is external to God, which is the world. The church cannot remain content with its inner diversity. It must also seek relations of irreducible difference beyond its sanctuary walls.

The text itself demands this. In Genesis 1:26-27, God said, "Let Us make man in Our image . . . in the image of God He created him." It is one image, but it is all humanity that mirrors that image. No one is left out. We have tended to see this text as indicating that each human being reflected the divine image. Why can't we see it as meaning that all humanity in its togetherness is a reflection of the divine image?

The Christian tradition has viewed the image as given, as lost, or severely damaged, and as potentially given again. That is, the image is portrayed as past and future. It is that which was given in creation, but it is that which calls us toward what can yet be. Was there an original unity to the human race in its infancy? How can we know? Is there a unity to the human race now? Everything we name as our unity is usually our shared characteristics, our DNA, our genetic mode of being. But this unity has never been enough to prevent us from trying to do away with one another, whether psychically, physically, or totally. I submit that it is not our unity that is God's image, but our communal being that is God's image, and this communal way of being is our call; it is yet before us; we have not yet achieved it.

The diversity within the church is one form of the image of God, but it remains to be completed by a deeper mode of diversity in community, and this is affirmation of religious pluralism. If "trinity" bespeaks irreducible differences, then surely religions themselves are irreducibly different. It is not the case that we are "all saying the same thing," or even that we all "worship the same God." Buddhists are a case in point; many forms of Buddhism do not worship any God. We are irreducibly diverse.

In the Christian notion of the Trinity, diversity is eternal. To model the Trinity throughout all of humanity, then, implies that each tradition must remain true to itself, essentially unlike the others, even as it continues its living development. We are called to become community together not by negotiating our differences, suppressing our differences, or by converting from our differences, but in and through our differences. We are called to become a community of diverse communities.

But how can this be? Let me take you to another set of Hebrew texts that flesh out a bit more what the image of God might be, not metaphysically, but morally. I take you a bit arbitrarily to the last six psalms, not because they are unique among all psalms or indeed all scripture, but simply because they are my favorites and because they give in awesome tones a further definition of God.

These remarkable writings are hymns alternating between prayer and praise expressed directly to God, and also expressed to one another within the human community. "Great is the LORD, and highly to be praised," begins these psalms, and "On the glorious splendor of Your majesty And on Your wonderful works, I will meditate" (145:3, 5). But the works that the psalmist then calls to mind are not works of awesome power in the way of Olympian thunderbolts and displays of omnipotence. Instead, the works are these: "The LORD is gracious and merciful; Slow to anger and great in lovingkindness. The LORD is good to all, And His mercies are over all His works. . . . The LORD sustains all who fall And raises up all who are bowed down. The eyes of all look to You, And You give them their food in due time. You open Your hand And satisfy the desire of every living thing" (145:8-9, 14-16). "[God] keeps faith forever; . . . executes justice for the oppressed; . . . gives food to the hungry . . . The LORD sets the prisoners free. The LORD opens *the eyes of* the blind; The LORD raises up those who are bowed down; The LORD loves the righteous; The LORD protects the strangers; He supports the fatherless and the widow, But He thwarts the way of the wicked" (146:6c-9). Words like these give us pause when we consider that to be human is to be created in the image of God. In the biblical text, this is the kind of God in whose image we are made, and presumably, then, these are the kinds of works in which we should engage, and the kinds of persons we are called to be, and the kinds of communities we should build.

To work toward the goal of becoming a community across lines of irreducible difference, after the model of the image of God, is to work according to the criterion of deeds of righteousness, mercy, and kindness. We become a communal image of God when we together discern and act on answers to these questions: Who is bowed down? Who are those without protection in society? How do we fill hungry stomachs, and abolish the needless structures of poverty? How do we deal with situations of imprisonment and torture? It is in looking toward works of mercy that can be done together that we actually become friends, community, and the image of God.[8]

In the nature of the case, of course, this image always calls us to new forms of expression. The image contains a restlessness within itself, for given our finite situation there is never a time when deeds of righteousness are unnecessary. Truly, we can do works of righteousness within our own communities, and this is right and good. But given the desperate needs in our world, we can do more together than we can do alone.

There are already places where religious people cooperate in deeds of mercy across religious lines. And there are organizations such as Amnesty International that draw persons from all and from no religious persuasions for the sake of doing good and undoing evil in arenas of political injustice. These are surely to be celebrated. I add this observation: As works of righteousness are undertaken cooperatively by institutions and persons of different religious persuasions, then something else is also going on. The image of God is being created in the world.

The Genesis text bespeaks not only a past, but a future in saying that we are created in the image of God. Insofar as that image is one of irreducibly diverse people joined together in communal efforts of righteousness, then the image is one that always calls us to ever-new instantiations. It is a call from our future. It requires more than a simple affirmation of our religious differences; it requires rejoicing in those differences and caring for one another across differences. Through them we can become a people who together create a shimmering image on earth of the God whose "nature and name is Love."

Questions for Reflection and Discussion

- How do you respond to the various ways theologians within the Christian tradition have tried to explain what "image of God" means? What have you thought it meant?

- What's your response to the argument that "image of God" is a communal term rather than an individual term—that it takes a community and not just an individual to mirror God's image?

- "Trinity" is a deeply Christian way of naming God. We are accustomed to the "Father, Son, Holy Spirit" naming of this Trinity, and one of our hymns speaks about "God in three persons, blessed Trinity."[9] How, then, do Christians escape from the notion that we worship three Gods?

- Traditionally, the unity of God has been named as love. This love is both internal, relating to the Divine Self, and external, relating to creation. Internally, God is an intensity of love whereby deepest complexity (threeness) is at the same time deepest unity (oneness). Do you think it possible for our church to be something like this? How would the church handle its internal differences if it were called to be an image of the Trinitarian God?

- Externally, the love of God calls creation into being. If there is diversity within God through Trinity, this diversity is carried to a great extreme through the otherness of creatures. To what extent does love require diversity?

- If we are to be an image of God's love toward others (toward us), must we ever be reaching toward those who are different from ourselves in some mode of love?

- Do you think it's possible that our being made in the image of God requires that we affirm those who are different from ourselves in attitudes and actions of love?

Tetsugen, a devotee of Zen in Japan, decided to publish the sutras, which at that time were available only in Chinese. The books were to be printed with wood blocks in an edition of seven thousand copies, a tremendous undertaking.

Tetsugen began by traveling and collecting donations for this purpose. A few sympathizers would give him a hundred pieces of gold, but most of the time he received only small coins. He thanked each donor with equal gratitude. After ten years Tetsugen had enough money to begin his task.

It happened that at that time the Uji River overflowed. Famine followed. Tetsugen took the funds he had collected for the books and spent them to save others from starvation. Then he began again his work of collecting.

Several years afterwards an epidemic spread over the country. Tetsugen again gave away what he had collected, to help his people.

For a third time he started his work, and after twenty years his wish was fulfilled. The printing blocks which produced the first edition of sutras can be seen today in the Obaku monastery in Kyoto.

The Japanese tell their children that Tetsugen made three sets of sutras, and that the first two invisible sets surpass even the last.[1]

CHAPTER FIVE

THE REIGN OF GOD

In these chapters I have explored the possibilities within Christianity for developing a theology that affirms religious pluralism. First, I have argued that a theology of creation based on the call and response process modeled in the first chapter of Genesis necessarily requires diversity within creation. If creation is covenantal, involving the world's response to God and God's response to the world, then the freedom of the world's response will be met by God's adaptation of the divine will toward the world's well-being in that time and place. As the Quakers are wont to say, "God is meet for our condition." God works with the freedom of the creature in diverse ways. And diverse communities of people develop as a result of the creative interaction between God and the world. We can affirm other religions because God has been at work calling them as well as ourselves into being.

Second, I developed this further by suggesting that God not only calls diverse religions into being, but that God is incarnate in these religions. This follows from probing the dynamics of a call and response creation. God's call comes not as something external to each finite existent, but as an influence received into each finite existent. Because this influence is toward the enactment of God's call toward inclusive well-being, those creatures who not only receive the call, but enact the call, witness to God's immanence in the world.

In the Christian tradition we call this form of immanence "incarnation," and have traditionally restricted it to Jesus Christ. But in process-relational theologies, God's immanence in the world comes to expression wherever God's call is actualized. Jesus is a revelation of the incarnational God through the wholeness of his response to God. This does not negate or eliminate other forms of God's immanence in the world. To the contrary, we take the revelation of God in Christ to be a witness of how God acts in the world. This radicalizes incarnation, saying that when God's aims are enacted anywhere, to that extent God is incarnate in the world. To follow this line of argument is to say that God not only calls various religions into being, but that God is manifested in these religions as well as in Christianity. *That* God is immanent in the world is given; *how* God is immanent depends upon the context.

My third development played with the notion of the image of God, again taking the Genesis texts as paradigmatic. A Christian understanding of the texts notes the plural usage in the text: "Let *Us* make man in *Our* image" (Gen. 1:26, emphasis added), and draws trinitarian conclusions. The God in whose image we are made is the triune God, named in our tradition as Father, Son, and Spirit. This Trinity is an irreducible diversity in deepest unity. The image of God, then, cannot be modeled by an individual alone; it can only be modeled by a community that is created through irreducibly diverse members.

Again, looking at the text, the whole of humanity is named as the image: "male and female [God] created them" (Gen. 1:27). Shall we not understand that it takes the whole of the human family, living in diverse ways but extending hands of friendship to one another, to be the image of God? The religions of the world are irreducibly diverse, with none being like the others even though there are things that all hold in common. The impossible possibility is that in our very diversity we are called to create a new kind of community in the world, where we respect one another's dignity and authenticity, and work together toward common good. We might yet be the image of God we were created to be and are still called to be.

In this chapter I suggest that the Christian symbol of "the reign of God" also gives us a theologically based reason for affirming other religions. This symbol extends further the criterion for evaluating ourselves and one another. I shall first show why this can be so, and then outline what I see to be some of the challenges of moving toward God's reign both in terms of dialogue, and in terms of cooperative action.

The Reign of God

While the reign of God is certainly intimated in Hebrew texts, it is dominant in the Christian Gospels. In what is probably our earliest Gospel, that according to Mark, the very first words attributed to Jesus are, "The time is fulfilled, and the kingdom of God is at hand; repent and believe in the gospel" (1:15). This inaugurates a three-year ministry of preaching, teaching, and healing in which Jesus both proclaims the reign of God, and embodies the reign of God.

The reign that Jesus preaches is continuous with Jewish history. We see this in his repetition of the deuteronomic command to love God with one's heart, soul, and strength, and one's neighbor as oneself. But most of all we see it in his living witness to what could be called the Hebrew scriptures' "litmus test" concerning God's call to human community. I dare say that there is not a society in the world that has not developed in and through its protection of its own way of being. In this process, structures emerge that work to the good of some, but not to the good of all. In every society, there are persons on the margins of the social good.

In the Hebrew scriptures, justice is tested by the extent to which society develops communal structures that channel well-being toward those with the least access to well-being. In the patriarchal society of ancient Israel, the least were typified by the widow and the orphan, neither of whom had the protection of husband or father. The stranger was also named as "least," for to be an alien in the society then as now was to be without the protections afforded to those who belonged to the society. Israel, in being called to be a righteous community, was called to see to the well-being of those who would otherwise meet misfortune. In passage after passage of the Hebrew scriptures, conformity to the command to love God and neighbor was measured by the community's kindness to those disadvantaged within the society, often typified as the widow, the orphan, and the stranger within one's gates.

Is such a situation so strange to us in our own societies? I live in California, where Mexico borders the southern portion of the state, and the wide Pacific forms the long coastal western border. California, with its twelve-month growing season, provides the produce for the supermarkets of America. But of course picking that produce is hard and demanding work; it does not require much knowledge of the English language, and while it may not pay well, at least it pays. Is it so strange, then, that Mexicans without employment in their own country should make their way over the border to pick the produce and earn a living? The problem, of course, is that immigration laws make this difficult, and so we have the phenomenon of the illegal alien in our state. The issue is not simply an issue with Mexicans; you may have heard of persons from China attempting to enter America in shipping containers that were never designed to transport people.

But these strangers within our gates are without the protection of American labor laws. For some, to arrive in America is to become entangled in virtual slavery, and it is hard to imagine that the situation encountered is any better than the situation left. The stranger is made an alien indeed, alienated and impoverished, without recourse to the normal channels of good in the society. We understand today how it was that Israel's righteousness—any nation's righteousness—can be measured by its treatment of the stranger within its gates.

To be kind to the stranger is to act counter to deeply ingrained human attitudes and fears. Think of it simply at the physiological level. Our bodies are constructed with a vast "distant early warning system" experienced as our immune reactions to any foreign substance. Obviously this is quite helpful, for we ward off many diseases through our cellular ability to isolate the strange organism and oust it. Our bodies create fevers so that they will become too hot and inhospitable for our more coolly adapted invaders! Indeed, our stratagems for fighting off unwelcome aliens can be carried to extremes. Too many of us have experienced a hyperactive immune system that cries, "Warning, warning!" in the presence of perfectly harmless plant pollens, causing us to reach for the antihistamine.

These physiological reactions to the stranger are mirrored in our societies. We are comfortable with our own kind, with those who share our values, with those who look like us. Our instinctive reactions to those unlike ourselves is to close in so that we might close them out. In the 1950s and 1960s Americans were beginning to stir from the evil sanction of Jim Crow laws, which were used against those of us whose ancestors had been enslaved. A society that had forced a whole people to become slaves punished them in their so-called freedom by keeping them in poverty, excluding them from educational opportunities, and preventing them from exercising their right to vote. Is it only a coincidence that when the Civil Rights movement began to stir, Hollywood suddenly began producing films about fearful invasions of aliens from outer space? Couldn't we read those films as the psychic consciousness of White people projecting their fears onto a cosmic screen? The message of the films was that to encounter one who is different is to encounter an alien who threatens, if not one's life, then one's lifestyle! And the answer to the alien is the killing fields, whether on a lynching tree or in bigger prisons.

To be human is to have a preference for one's own kind; we do not much like the stranger within our gates. Yet the ancient call to justice measures our societies precisely by how we treat those whom we like the least, the strangers. Jesus preached and lived this message. In his own day the stranger was the hated Roman, the Samaritans, the Syrophoenicians, and within Israel itself, the leper. Anyone who knows those Gospels can immediately call to mind story after story, even as told to our Sunday school children, of Jesus going to the Roman centurion's house, talking with the Samaritan woman, healing the Syrophoenician's daughter, cleansing the lepers. Well-being is extended to the stranger within the gates. Matthew 25 culminates that Gospel's rapid succession of reign-of-God parables and messages. There the writer presents the judgment scene of God's reign with the litany of the least. Included in this litany, of course, is the ancient test of the stranger: "I was a stranger," Jesus says, "and you invited Me in" (v. 34).

The care of God is universal, and therefore none are to be excluded from participation in the good of the community. In this vein, the reign of God as preached by Jesus called for a "reversal of values." Long-standing assumptions are to be raised to the critical question of how our societies do and do not create a system of care that extends to all. A metaphor for the situation is found in our irrigated fields. The central valley of California is prime agricultural country, but rainfall is sparse. To drive through the valley is to see mile after mile of fields and orchards, each with its carefully designed irrigation system ensuring that no part of the field is without adequate water. Even so, societies must see to their own "irrigation fields" to ensure that access to the well-being afforded within that society is available to all. The shortcomings of the society are measured by the well-being—or ill-being—of those least likely to participate in society's benefits. These are those who are named as least, or whoever is today's equivalent of the widow, the orphan, and the stranger within our gates. They are the measure of the society's success or failure.

The Contemporary Call

The church of Jesus Christ is called to heed his call to a reign of God measured by inclusive well-being. This requires a constant self-critique within every society, always according to the test of justice. Established norms are to be subjected to the question of the marginalized, and readjusted accordingly. Because the tendency of every society is to develop and sanctify particular patterns of well-being, and because it is the nature of human society to codify its norms, and because no matter how just a society might be today, its tomorrow will yield a new form of the marginalized—"you always have the poor with you" (Matt. 26:11; Mark 14:7; John 12:8)—the reign of God is a principle of unrest continuously calling a society to its own reform. We are marked by a tendency to value our own kind more highly than we value those perceived as other. We are called to transcend this natural tendency by cultivating forms of spirituality that are governed by love toward God and neighbor. We are called continuously to the reign of God.

The Reign of God and Religious Pluralism

And what does this brief discussion of the reign of God have to do with our topic of religious pluralism? Within Christianity, our proclivity for valuing our own kind meets its ultimate test in relation to those whose religious ways are not our own—those strangers who are now indeed "within our gates" in this increasingly small world. In our history, we have often demanded conversion as the test of community. Our historic Christian missionary activity was primarily for the sake of conversion, so that too often (certainly not always) even the sharing of social goods and ministering to physical needs that accompanied mission activity was used to pave the way for the ultimate goal of religious conversion. We have too often extended well-being to the other in the hope that the other will, in fact, become like us.

Against this tendency, we must look again to the criterion of the stranger. The stranger is not one who comes among us unknown, but then turns out to be just like us. Nor is the stranger one who changes his or her ways in order to become like us. The stranger is precisely that: a stranger whose way of life differs from our own, and who remains committed to this alternative way. The stranger, by definition, is different from ourselves.[2]

Does this not describe the category of religions other than one's own? Are not those whose mode of spirituality differs from our own, those whose worship may not even be to the same God, or indeed, to any god; those whose ethics follow different patterns, are not these persons and societies strangers to us? Are not all the religions of the world strangers to one another? In our situations of mass migrations, these strangers are indeed now within one another's gates.

Shall we leave off the ancient litmus test of the reign of God? Or, rather, shall we think of new ways to apply it in these new situations in which we find ourselves? How can we live toward the reign of God by regarding well the strangers within our gates, within our world?

Perhaps our two thousand-year history of attempting in various ways and to various degrees to live according to the reign of God is now being drawn to a new and ultimate reversal of values: to extend well-being to those whom we neither require nor expect to become like ourselves. We have struggled as a church to be a community that witnesses to the reign of God in the world, and for many years we understood this witness to be for the sake of conversion. But if the reign of God is always a principle of unrest, daring us to reverse previous values for the sake of greater well-being, then the reign of God is that which always calls us to dare a new future. It is a frightening thing sometimes to let go of long-established ways of being in order that a new good might come about. But if it is God's reign that calls us, then trust in the God who calls us gives us strength to reach toward the new future. Perhaps we are now called to become a community that witnesses to the reign of God in the world for the sake of friendship, through which we all might turn the world itself into a community of communities.

Differences, especially religious differences, need not be the occasion for hostilities and wars, but may become the occasion for friendship, where we each reach out to the other, the stranger. Difference, otherness, invites respect and friendship, rather than fear, defensiveness, and injustice.

The argument against this, of course, is the irony that religious differences have often been major instigators of war. Our demand for own-kindness, and either our fear or jealousy or both of those we name as other, have been fueled by religion. But this is precisely why religions themselves are key to transcending the prevailing norm of "own-kindness."

This particular time in our long cultural evolution as people of the world may be absolutely crucial to our continuing or not continuing the human saga. We have grown beyond our ability to sustain insulated communities, unaffected by one another. Surely the recently completed century, with its genocides, hatreds, and forms of destruction and violence unprecedented in all human history witnesses to our need to grow beyond the ugliness of valuing only our "own kind"! Our twenty-first century threatens to add to the terror wreaked by "own-kindness" unless we can change our ways. I suggest that God is drawing Christians into the challenge of learning how to be part of a larger world community of diverse communities. A theology of the reign of God calls us toward a new affirmation of religious pluralism.

The Challenge

How do we begin such a reversal of values? Practically speaking, how do we reach out to the strangers within our gates? We have been tentatively moving beyond our preference for "own-kindness" through the means of interreligious dialogue ever since the Second World War, when the horror of the Holocaust prompted us to think it advisable to begin serious dialogue between Christians and Jews. At the present time there are a variety of conversations occurring around the globe as persons from various religious communities meet with one another for the sake of mutual understanding. I suggest that these dialogues may indeed be the result of God's calls to live from and toward God's reign.

But dialogue is not easy, and some questions concerning conflicting truth claims and conflicting value systems that have been raised come to the fore when we move from considering other religions abstractly, toward meeting persons from those traditions concretely. And the issues are not minor. Perhaps the hardest issues to overcome are not contradictory ideas of God, but contradictory values, such as the role of women. These issues represent an area of profound disagreement both within and among religions.

The affirmation of religious pluralism, as I have outlined it in these essays, recognizes the root of all our concepts in culture, and the intertwining of our ethics with our cultures as developed over centuries. On the one hand this relativizes our value systems. They are peculiar to their origins. But it most surely does not eliminate our value systems. Furthermore, since God has called us into being, we are to honor the value systems that are entailed in our respective religions, whether it is the Christian tradition or any other tradition, in a critical and open way.

That is, since the reign of God is a principle of unrest calling us to deeper forms of inclusive well-being, we must always subject our value systems to the critique of that criterion. We do not hold our values in an absolute way, but in a critical way.

In part, this critical openness recognizes that our values reflect our various human responses as well as the call of God. How do we know that a particular value is not more akin to the prejudice of what I have called "own-kindness" rather than the call of God? Thus, we are to hold the values that are woven into who we are in a mode of critical openness; they are mixtures of God's call and human responsiveness in the complex evolution of one's religious culture. The criterion to which they are held is inclusiveness of well-being in the human and earthly community. Within the Christian tradition, the application of that norm has led to a radical revision of its centuries' old subordination of women.

So, then, what of this dialogue between the Christian and those of other religions who hold quite different values? If I see what appears to be the oppression of women within any system, can I enter into open dialogue? Because the other is the "stranger within my gates," and because this other's social structure depends upon the oppression of women, do I suppress my Christian values? Do I honor the other by keeping quiet about my own commitments?

Let me return to the model of friendship. Friendships develop not because one friend suppresses who she or he really is, but because one expresses who one is. Friendship depends upon an honesty of relationship, even, and perhaps especially, in one's differences. Because we are friends, we can speak our minds to each other. The friendship is deeper than our differences, and we offer each other respect and dignity whether we agree or not.

The same applies to friendship across religious communities. The call of the reign of God compels me to respect this stranger who is in dialogue with me, even as I speak from my own value system. Because I am convinced that God calls us to inclusive well-being, and because the oppression of women violates inclusive well-being, I quite openly think that oppression of women in any system (including my own!) is wrong. I also consider such oppression a reflection of human responses to protect "own-kindness" against the perceived other, rather than a response to the direct call of God. I cannot conceive of oppression of any type as a reflection of the incarnate God, whether within Christianity or any other system.

But the call of the gospel calls me to refrain from demonizing this one with whom I ardently disagree. To the contrary, I am called to listen even as I speak. I might even hear the other ask what the church is doing to alleviate the condition of the strangers within America's gates, for the same criterion I hold relative to the other is one I must apply to Christianity.

Friendship toward the one who differs religiously does not call for a suspension of one's values; to the contrary, it calls for speaking one's values, and hearing the values of another. It calls for attempts at mutual understanding. Further, just as my outsider's view gives me a certain perspective on another's situation, it is so that the stranger's views offer a distinct perspective on my situation. It could be that I will learn more about my own Christianity in dialogue with this other than I ever could when my conversational partners are restricted to those who are like me.

Will Dialogue Change Us?

Because we learn from one another in dialogue, some theologians are convinced that dialogue is but one step in the process of affirming other religions. As I noted in chapter 1, John B. Cobb Jr.'s thesis is that by hearing the worldviews of others, one is led to truths not available through the lens of one's own religion. Another theologian, Jay McDaniel, published *With Roots and Wings: Christianity in an Age of Ecology and Dialogue,*[3] with a similar thesis. Both argue that since all things human, including religions, are in flux, the question is not *whether* religions will change, but *how* they will change. Interreligious dialogue affects the ways in which religions change. To risk dialogue is to risk openness to unexpected transformations, to the point that McDaniel names himself a "Buddhist Christian." By this, he means that he has integrated Buddhist insights into his own spiritual life as a Christian.

There are far-reaching implications for a theory like this. I have argued that a theology of the reign of God calls us toward extending hands of friendship to the strangers, to other religions. And I have also argued that irreducible diversity is essential to the fullness of the image of God, so that we are being led not to a single world community in which all differences are downplayed, but toward a different form of community that itself is composed of irreducibly different communities. The model of friendship rather than conformity applies to this model.

And yet friendships can change us. In personal relationships, we see this as good: friendships enrich us, give us wider concerns, open us to new wisdom. And yet friendships flourish most when we can be our deepest selves within the friendship. Can this not also be the case in friendships between religious communities?

Perhaps an old story that I learned from rabbinic Judaism tells it best. An impoverished, devout rabbi named Jacob ben Josef lived in the Krakow ghetto in a dwelling that was little more than a roof over dirt floor, a stove, and a mat. One night the rabbi had a strange dream: The Lord told him to travel to Prague, where he would find a bridge over the river. He was to dig under the northwest corner of the bridge, and there he would find a treasure that would allow him to build a house of prayer and to give many alms. Clearly the message was but a dream, so the rabbi ignored it. A second night the same dream came, and again the rabbi ignored it. But when it came the third night as well, the good man packed up a few belongings and began the long and arduous journey to Prague. After many days of hardship he arrived, only to discover that the Lord had failed to mention the great burly guard whose guardhouse was built precisely at the northwest corner of the bridge! The rabbi hardly knew what to do, so for several days he paced back and forth trying to figure it out. The guard noticed the poor fellow, and challenged him: "What is your business?" The honest man told him about the perplexing thrice-repeated dream, at which the guard roared in laughter. "Why you foolish man," said he, "you have journeyed all this way for a mere dream? Hah! If I believed in dreams I would have traveled all the way to some nonde-script ghetto in the city of Krakow and inquired where a Jew named Jacob ben Josef lived. Can you imagine! To a ghetto, where half the Jews are named Jacob and the other half are named Josef! And then I should have gone to the miserable dwelling of this Jew, dug under his stove, and found myself a great treasure! But am I so stupid as to believe in such a wild goose of a dream? Not me! Go home, you old fool, begone with you!" And so Rabbi Jacob ben Josef bowed, thanked the man most humbly, journeyed home, moved his stove, and began to dig. And the treasure was so great that he built a fine house of prayer, and provided food for many years for the poor.

Sometimes one must travel to a far country to find the riches that exist in one's own home, under one's own hearth, in the warmth of one's own fires. Traveling into the ways of another religion can allow us to see our own ways with a new perspective, revealing riches to us that we'd forgotten we had. Perhaps we will gain the novelty of a new perspective on old insights. Our encounters with other religions—and other cultures—might allow us to remove to some degree (though not completely) our American cultural glasses to look again at the gospel of Jesus Christ. And what we see through the eyes of the other might be treasures already hidden beneath our own hearths.

This is not to say that dialogue cannot transform us. But its first impact may well be to transform us through fresh insights into our own religion. And that abiding principle of unrest, the reign of God that calls us to deeper modes of inclusive well-being—deeper modes of love—can renew our insight and transform our ways of developing and expressing and living our faith. The criterion will be toward richer forms of human community.

A theology of the reign of God can lead us to dare encountering the stranger, those of other religions. This encounter will be reaching out in friendship, and the friendship itself will be expressed in modes of dialogue and in works of mercy. Dialogue will not only give us an understanding of the other, it can give us a deeper understanding of ourselves. Interreligious dialogue, and indeed, the diversity required in the image of God and the reign of God, calls upon us not to a superficial Christianity, but to a deep Christianity. We must know ourselves historically and culturally, and offer this truth that is ourselves to the other in friendship. From the sureness of our Christianity, we are called to be open to the sureness of the stranger as well.

Can this happen? Can we, as Christians, affirm other religions as works of God in other cultures that we are to respect? Can we understand the God of creation to be the God of all creation, working with stories not our own, but working faithfully according to the divine nature? Can we see that the incarnation we have recognized in Jesus Christ means that God is one who works immanently within the world, and therefore is also manifest in the world in a variety of ways? Can we who are Christian, who understand God as the irreducible diversity-in-unity that we name as Trinity, dare to become the image of this God through friendship with those who are irreducibly different from us? And finally, can we dare to live a reign of God that reaches not toward an imperialism of one religion—our own!—sweeping the planet, but that reaches toward a new form of community; a community made up of diverse religious communities, existing together in friendship?

Perhaps it is indeed so that to answer all these questions in the affir-

mative will lead us toward transformation. Traditions, after all, are created in and through their own transformation. The critical point is
whether the transfomation is internally chosen or externally imposed.
New insight gleaned from strangers can lead to transformation that is
deeply Christian, calling us beyond our present state in conformity with
the reign of God. As friends with one another, religious people around
the world can be called to the transformation of working together rather
than against one another. We can be called to value our differences, and
to value well-being in broader modes than that presently attained. For we
will be called to look to the well-being of all marginalized people; we will
be called to look to the well-being of our earth. When this happens, to
whatever degree, perhaps there will be a new shimmering on this planet.
Perhaps, just perhaps, there will be a glow that is indeed the image of God
reflected from us all, and deeds of love and mercy that are direct answers
to that ancient prayer, "thy kingdom come."

Questions for Reflection and Discussion

- What is the religion other than your own that you know the
  most? How is it that you know of this religion? Did you once
  share it? Did you study it academically? Do you know it because
  of friends who belong to this religion?

- How do you see God in this religion? Where do you think God
  is *not* revealed in this religion? What criterion do you use? How
  did you develop this criterion?

- How is it possible to honor God in another religion, and at the
  same time honor God as understood through your own tradition?

- Is it possible to discuss ethical differences with those who think
  differently? Think first of how we discuss these differences
  within our own community. Since these intrareligious differences are difficult, how, then, do we discuss interreligious differences?

- Is it a positive or negative thing that friendships can change us?
  How do we deal with this religiously?

- How do *you* apply "the reign of God" to religious pluralism?

Two monks from China were making a pilgrimage to India to visit the shrines of Buddhism. But the way was long and the path difficult; it was a journey taking many months. As they went through a remote village, still in China, they were overcome with weariness and thirst. An old woman took pity on them, gave them water, and invited them to rest a while in her poor hut.

"Ah," they said, "would that we had something to give you to repay you for your kindness! On our return journey, we will bring you a relic of the Buddha to show our gratitude." The woman thanked them profusely, and they went on their way. Many long months later they made the return journey, and as they approached the village they remembered in alarm their promise to the woman.

"Here," said one, "look at this!" The skeleton of a dog lay by the side of the road. "Let us take a tooth and give it to her as if it were the Buddha's tooth." And so they did, and when they gave it to the woman she received it gladly, for she was very devout. She set the tooth in the very center of her small shrine.

Several years later the monks once again set out on pilgrimage. This time, as they approached the woman's village, they noticed a soft glow over the woman's hut. When they looked in the door they were astonished to see that the dog's tooth was the source of the glow, for it had become golden, emitting a radiance that filled the humble dwelling. Then the monks looked at each other and smiled, saying, "Her faith has made it so."

—a Buddhist story from China

CHAPTER SIX

SAVING GRACE

Review: Four Images

The four Christian images of creation through call and response, radical incarnation, the image of God, and the Reign of God can all be interpreted in ways that support Christian acceptance of religious pluralism. God creates through a call and response whose effects we can trace through evolution. The freedom of the world in its multitude of responses accounts for the vast diversity within the world. We trust that God in faithfulness works continuously in and through that diversity to bring creation not only into being, but toward modes of community that embrace difference.

And we Christians know more than most people that God works incarnationally. We celebrate incarnation not only at Christmas, but throughout our Christian lives. God is not a remote God, far removed from creation. To the contrary, God is with us in the midst of things, a very present help because God is a very near help. God works through cultures, even though that necessarily means God also works *despite* cultures. And if the whole developing Christian tradition is a witness that God can work through Mediterranean cultures, Greco-Roman cultures, European cultures, Indian cultures, Asian cultures, African cultures, and American cultures, is it so strange to assert that God works in and through cultures not only for Christians, but for all people?

God works not in random ways, but in purposeful ways. The Christian doctrine of creation in the image of God argues that the purpose of God's work in creation and culture is to draw finite existence toward becoming an image of God. To be an image of God is to enact within our finite circumstances the infinite love of God. As Christians, we name God as Triune. This speaks to depths of divine love, such that within God's self God is infinitely communal and infinite love. And the love that is within God is not jealously hoarded. Rather, out of love, God creates a true other, a world, in order that the world shall be in its own way an image of God. Perhaps it takes eons, perhaps, given the freedom of the world, we only grope and stumble toward becoming that image. But God's purposes in creation urge us toward exercising love toward one another, despite our deepest differences. Creation in the image of God requires diversity within creation in order that the love we give, like God's, shall reach toward otherness for the sake of love, of community.

And the ancient image of the Reign of God reinforces this. What is added by this image is the emphasis that love is not to be given only to those who are like us, but that love is evoked by and offered to the stranger. We are all strangers in some context or other, and we know what it is to be needy. If the creative purpose of God is to draw us toward the divine image of love, that very image requires us to love those who are unlike ourselves. The Reign of God draws the whole world toward a breadth of community hitherto unknown: a world community of peace, a "peaceable kingdom."

The Cross

And yet, is there not a major problem? Central to our Christian faith is the image of a cross and a resurrection. The dominant tradition within Christianity is the view that the incarnation of God in Christ is for the sake of drawing the sins of the world into Christ's own self, paying the penalty for sin, clearing the way to God. But if Christ clears the way to God, is not Christianity the ultimate religion? Some have argued that because all humans are blocked from God by sin, the only way to God is through the One who takes that sin from us. Perhaps, they have said, it's so that there are people in all religions who seem to be well-pleasing to

God, and by their fruits we know them. But maybe in some post-life existence they will realize that it is Jesus they have believed in all along. Or perhaps they have a chance to acknowledge Jesus in some post-life state, so that finally they, too, are redeemed by Christ.

C. S. Lewis gives a beautiful image of this in *The Last Battle*, his final Narnian book for children. Aslan represents Christ in this series, and Tash is the name given to a false god who masquerades as good, but who actually wills evil. A young boy who has grown up in a land devoted to the worship of Tash misunderstands the character of Tash, attributing to Tash qualities that actually characterize Aslan. In a final battle between good and evil, the boy valiantly fights for Tash. He is brokenhearted when Tash is defeated by the forces of Aslan. Then all creation slowly passes by Aslan to receive judgment. The sobbing boy joins the line, dreading the sight of Aslan. But when he reaches him, and raises his eyes, he is astonished by joy. There, before him, is the one he has unwittingly loved all along. He is one of the redeemed.

Such a story is comforting to the Christian assertion that Christianity alone offers the ultimate in salvation to which all must finally yield. But it wreaks havoc with the notion of religious pluralism. It allows a seeming and temporary pluralism, although Christianity finally triumphs as the one true faith. All will eventually become Christian, or realize the dreadful consequences of being separated from God forever. There is no real pluralism.

Is it the case, then, that all pluralism finally falters on the issue of how saving grace is given to the world? Must we understand the Cross and Resurrection in such a way that unless one is united with Christ in death and resurrection, there is no way to God? Let us look more closely at the tradition to see where it can take us. The pieces to be dealt with are as follows: the role of Adam, the rise in Israel of the notion of resurrection, criminal death as expiatory, and the importance of the Cross and Resurrection. I ask your patience as we deal with each of these pieces, and then see how they were variously woven together throughout Christian history. This brief study prepares the way for a genuinely pluralistic understanding of saving grace.

The Role of Adam

Have you ever wondered about the importance of Adam in the New Testament and in Christian theology? Have you not considered the conundrum that Adam is not at all important in any Old Testament book save for those two chapters in Genesis? Have you noticed that he is never mentioned again, neither in the Old Testament books nor in the Gospels, until you get to the Epistles? Why does Adam then become important?

One of the problems with the story of Adam is that we read it as the beginning of the story, when in fact Adam actually comes in the middle of the story. Because it is placed early in Genesis, we assume—whether consciously or not—that Adam starts the whole thing. But he doesn't. Genesis is not the first book of the Bible to be written. The prophetic books, which Christians (not Jews) place at the end of the Old Testament, were written prior to Genesis. Interpreters of Genesis argue that within the Hebrew scriptures, the story of Adam is not an account of the human fall into evil; to the contrary, it is an account of maturation. But in a sense this is immaterial to the Christian tradition, where Adam was understood to be an answer to the question, "Why is there evil in the world?"

Move yourself imaginatively into the ancient world. Erase from your knowledge (if possible) contemporary theories of biology and the other sciences, and move into ancient biology. How are humans reproduced? For Aristotle, it was clear that the male principle is the generative principle; the woman is but the material principle. The woman receives the seed, but is unable to cause it to take shape. This action belongs to the male principle, now nourished within the female body to become a new human being.[1] The female contributes the material that the soul then fashions into shape. Thus, the soul derives from the man, while the matter is derived from the woman. Christian theologians, accepting this theory of reproduction, then naturally understood that the very first human being, Adam, contained within his testes the potential souls of all people who would ever live. These potential souls would be passed on to every son, first through Adam, and subsequently, of course, through the successive sons who would be born in due time. All persons who ever lived were present, then, within Adam.

The story is familiar. Adam is created perfect, and in order to exhibit his perfection, he is given one easily obeyed task. He is not to eat fruit from the tree of the knowledge of good and evil, for when he does, he will die. And of course he eats it. It's not really possible for him *not* to eat it, for remember that the story is developed by Christian theologians in order to explain why we have evil. One starts the adamic story from the known conclusion—we have evil in the world—and works backward to explain why. Adam must disobey God in order to explain evil. And as mentioned in chapter 4, when he disobeys he loses the fullness of the divine image in which he was created.

Consider the situation. How much of Adam sinned? Were his finger-nails involved in his Fall? The question seems silly, until you think about the biology. It is ridiculous to think that although Adam fell, there were some parts of him that were unaffected by the Fall. Therefore, all those potential souls were just as involved in Adam's fall as the rest of him, it was the whole human being, Adam, who disobeyed God, not just some part of him. Therefore, when Adam lost the divine image and became plunged into guilt and death, all those future souls were likewise affected. So then, everyone who is born of Adam is tainted by Adam's original sin, bearing Adam's guilt. We are all born toward sin and death. And that explains, said the ancients, why we have sin and evil in the world. Augustine, for example, held that evil is the result of sin and its punishment.

Now ask yourself why virgin birth was important in Christianity, and the answer becomes obvious. Remember, the woman contributed nothing generative to the soul; hers was but the passive material that the new soul would use. If Jesus was born from a male's seed, he too would have been in Adam, sharing Adam's guilt, and like the rest of us, would need redemption. Thus Jesus had to be born of a virgin from a wholly new soul that was never present in Adam.[2]

It's not clear that the apostle Paul worked with this biology, for virgin birth is not important in the writings of Paul. But he does see Adam as the head of the race, whose transgression plunges the race he represents into sin and death. By contrast, Christ's righteousness provides a new start, with justification and life. This is what makes him a second Adam, and it is why Paul develops a parallel between Adam and Jesus. Adam is the head of the race by generation, so that everyone who lives or has lived has by definition been tainted by Adam. Everybody shares in the guilt of his sin. But Jesus offers a new opportunity. He is the new head of the race, not now by physical generation, but by spiritual regeneration. The problem, then, is how we can transfer our belonging to Adam to belonging to Christ. In Adam, we die, but if we can be united with Christ, then in him there can be a great reversal of Adam's death, and we can live. How this can be accomplished is a complex story, requiring digression into two interesting segments of ancient Jewish history. The first deals with the origins of the belief in resurrection, and the second has to do with criminal deaths.

The Origins of the Notion of Resurrection

Christians have often noted that Israel was frequently enmeshed in warfare, with other people constantly invading Israel. Any look at a map can tell you why. Little Israel was like a buffer zone between the great nations of the ancient world. When these nations fought, Israel was often the battlefield. It was the genius of the Jews to interpret this situation religiously. God must be punishing them for their sins, they thought. They turned their misfortunes into opportunities to learn to be more just, and to judge themselves according to the well-being of the least in their communities. Since every nation in the world can always find instances of injustice within its borders, it's not surprising that Israel could always point to some sin or other that was responsible for the punishment being inflicted upon them by God through these great invading nations.

But the books of Job and Habakkuk begin to question this theory. Job raises the question of personal suffering, and Habakkuk raises the question of social suffering. Habakkuk stands on the watchtower as the enemies approach once more to destroy the tiny nation, and Habakkuk probes the conscience of the nation, asking for which committed sin they are about to be punished. In the process, he considers the morals of the invaders. "God," he says, "you may be using this people to punish us, but have you seen how *they* act? What's going on?" The theory of war-as-God-punishing-us-for-sin was beginning to break down.

The final blow to the theory came in the time of the Maccabees. Once again the people had been invaded, this time by the Greeks. The conquering people insisted on their own culture as superior to the Jewish culture, imposing Greek ways on the Jewish nation. To an extent, the Jewish people accepted the yoke of the conqueror, until the conqueror decided that in order fully to crush the Jews, the Jewish Holy of Holies must be defiled. "*No!*" answered the Jews, led by the Maccabean priests. The priests valiantly defended the Temple, willing to die rather than to desecrate God's Temple—and die they did. But with their deaths, the old theories finally crumbled. The Maccabees were righteous, so righteous that they died rather than disobey God. How could their deaths be seen as just? Does not God reward righteousness? Rather than relinquish trust in the righteousness of God, the Jews drew the obvious conclusion. The Maccabees were not vindicated in this life, but God *is* a God of justice. Therefore, there must be more than this life. And the belief in the resurrection was born as the vindication of the righteous judgment of God.[3]

Expiatory Punishment

The next piece in the story emerges through the horrible practices of crucifixion in the Roman world. This miserable form of death was blasphemous to the Jews, for whom burial was deeply important. In crucifixion, the Romans not only nailed thousands of persons to crosses, but they left them there to rot. It was a dreaded form of death. Remember that Judaism was still a sacrificial system—not of human sacrifice, which God clearly forbade in the story of Abraham and Isaac. Offerings of birds or animals on the Temple altars atoned for sin and guilt. But the death by crucifixion was like an ultimate sacrifice. And so the custom arose that upon crucifixion the prisoner would utter the ritualistic words, "With my death I atone for all my sins."[4]

The Death and Resurrection of Jesus

Weave these elements together, and you can begin to see the emergence of Christian soteriology, the Christian doctrine of salvation. Jesus, like the Maccabees, was righteous. "Which of you convicts me of sin?" is recorded in the gospel, and the answer is "None." There is no place within the Gospels where Jesus is in any way connected with personal sin. In no way, then, can his death be interpreted as an atonement for his own sin. For whom, then, can this death avail? Furthermore, if God is righteous, and if Jesus reveals through his whole life the very righteousness of God, must it not be the case that God cannot leave him in the grave? God's justice must be vindicated in the resurrection of this wholly righteous man.

Now weave this onto the story of Adam, which rose to new prominence in the intertestamental times and was picked up by Paul in relation to Christ. Adam, as the representative of the race, sins. For Paul, Adam, as the first man, was the designated representative of us all, much as a king represents the whole people. Our plight, then, is that under Adam we were sold into sin and death. And it's not just that we have this inherited problem. We manage quite well to invent our own peculiar ways of sinning. So, then, we are sinners first on account of Adam, and then on account of our own sinful acts. Sin naturally brings about punishment; in fact, it brings the punishment of death. This is not arbitrary, for sin separates us from the holy God, and God is the source of all life. To be separated from God is to be a creature toward death. What we need is another Adam, one who helps us to start over, first by taking care of the problem of sin's consequences, and second, by enabling us to live righteously.

Jesus is that second Adam who, unlike the first Adam, fulfills the whole law. He incurs no death penalty for himself. Nevertheless, we kill him in a horrible way. Given his own righteousness, that death is gratuitously applied to those who have merited death, which is to say, to every child of Adam. In Adam we die, but in the second Adam, we can be made alive.

But how are we to take advantage of this new opportunity? The fateful participation in Adam is simply a given, whether by representation, as for Paul, or by biology, as for the later theologians such as Augustine. Jesus has no physical children; how do we participate in him? And the answer is by faith. By trusting that God has dealt with our sin in Jesus' death, we unite ourselves with Christ by faith. His death then becomes our death. And if we die with him, we are also raised with him to newness of life. The barrier between us and God—our sin and its consequences—is torn down. God's love flows into us, and we are freed to live a resurrection life.

These are the broad outlines, then, of why Jesus' death and resurrection are absolutely central to our Christian faith. Our problem is that because of our association with Adam, we are sinners, and sin entails death by virtue of its separation from the holy God. But there is a second Adam, one who is outside the first Adam and therefore not associated with sin either through Adam or through his own deeds. His death is therefore not for himself, but for us. By faith we can be united with this second Adam. This bridges the separation caused by sin, reunites us with God, and makes it possible for us to live as God intended in lives of love. To live from love is to be righteous; it is to live anew; it is to be resurrected from the death of sin here in this life, and eventually in the life to come.

Four Soteriologies

There have been many variations on the above themes within the history of Christian attempts to understand exactly what God has done for us in Christ. In a sense, Christians already *have* a pluralistic soteriology— or at least a pluralism of soteriologies! The issue is, How does union with Christ by faith solve our problem of enmeshment in sin? *That* this union saves us is not in question; *how* it saves us is. Again, a look back at

Christian history becomes instructive, for four primary "how's" have been identified through the ages. Each one depends upon slight differences in naming our problem.

Most persons in the early centuries of Christianity named mortality as our major problem. Remember, it was an age of high infant mortality and short life spans. Why? Sin requires punishment, and the punishment is death. Since all were inside the sinning Adam, all must die. How can the death of the innocent Jesus be justly transferred to us, so that his death suffices for our own? How can we gain immortality, despite our sin? What Gustaf Aulén called the "dramatic theory of the atonement" became an answer.[5] The theory requires the introduction of a new player in the drama—Satan—and it presupposes a cosmic prologue wherein a good angel spontaneously decides to defy God.[6] This angel's defection gives this creature sovereignty over the realm of sin and death. When Adam sins, therefore, he and all his progeny automatically enter the kingdom of Satan and become subject to death.

But only those who are descended from Adam belong justly to this kingdom. Since Jesus is neither descended from Adam nor is he a sinner, he does not belong to the kingdom of Satan nor does he merit death. If Satan takes Jesus in death, he violates cosmic law. Augustine uses the imagery of a "mousetrap" and of a "fishhook" to describe what happens next. God tempts Satan to take Jesus in death anyhow by arranging the crucifixion. Only if Satan takes Jesus will he die, because Jesus has no tendency to death within himself. Satan, knowing that Jesus is God incarnate, sees his crucifixion as a once-in-creation opportunity to triumph over his enemy by taking Jesus/God in death! So he pounces on the bait, and swallows Jesus up in death. The trick, of course, is that Jesus cannot be held by death because of his righteousness. He is resurrected in triumph. But because he has been taken unjustly, Satan must pay the forfeit not only of releasing Jesus, but also of releasing those who are connected to Jesus by faith, which is conferred graciously and sacramentally in and through baptism. Consequently, the answer to the problem of sin and mortality comes about through our union with Christ, through whom we, too, participate in Christ's defeat of the devil.

In the Middle Ages a somewhat different way of understanding how and why God saves us developed. The basic problem of our identification with Adam remained. But the problem of our sin was no longer the problem of mortality, it was the problem of having dishonored God. In a feudalistic society, serfs owed absolute fidelity to their liege lord. To fail in this fidelity was to dishonor the lord, and to be subject to a penalty that would render satisfaction for the particular insult. Late in the eleventh century Anselm of Canterbury developed an intriguing theory of why God became incarnate in Jesus, which reflected this feudal situation. By sinning, Adam (and hence all humankind) had not rendered appropriate honor to God. Unfortunately for humans, in dishonoring the infinite God they had incurred an infinite debt, requiring infinite satisfaction. But how could a merely finite being offer infinite satisfaction? The problem was insoluble. Since a finite being had given the dishonor, a finite being must render satisfaction. But since an infinite being had been dishonored, only an infinite satisfaction would do. But by definition, no finite being could render an infinite satisfaction! The answer to the conundrum, of course, was incarnation. If God became human, conjoining human nature and divine nature in one individual, then a finite being would be able to render infinite satisfaction! So God did this, and by God's gracious act, all who are united with this finite/infinite being—this Christ—by faith are counted to have rendered the satisfaction due to the Lord of lords.[7]

Peter Abelard, in the twelfth century, developed yet another theory. For Abelard, our problem is primarily our ignorance, which trapped us in sin and its punishment. Because our minds are darkened by sin, we have but a dim apprehension of the way God would have us live. To overcome this problem, God became incarnate so that we could see, in the living man Jesus, how it is that we might respond to God's love for us through our own responsive love to God and neighbor. By becoming united with Jesus in and through faith, his example illumines us. Christ becomes our teacher, and also our mediator, constantly praying for us. Through Christ, then, we are rescued from our ignorance, and made capable of holy living. For Abelard, the life of Christ assumes a new importance. In earlier theories, Christ's life was important primarily to establish his sinlessness, without which he would have merited death. But for Abelard, Christ's life is important for what it teaches us concerning holy living in response to God's love.[8]

Yet another variation emerged during the Reformation. This time the problem was unbelief—and this, in turn, meant that we are devoid of the faith that unites us with Christ. This separation from Christ is dire, since only through him can we be freed from the punishment we deserve for our original sin in Adam, and the personal sins we have added to that debt. God's justice demands that we all pay the punishment of death. The sinless Jesus dies. Because of his sinlessness, he deserves no punishment. Therefore, he undertakes the punishment of death on our behalf. In effect, he pays the sentence that we deserve. In God's law court of perfect justice, Jesus is our substitute. All that God now requires of us is faith in

God's own promise that we are made acceptable in and through Christ. Our sins are stamped, "punishment paid."

These four major interpretations of just why it is that Jesus' death saves us have been presented in many variations throughout our two millennia. In three of the four, the basic issue revolves around some form of substitution whereby what Jesus does is transferred to us. Each of these three is characterized by a "great exchange." Our plight is passed to Jesus, and his resolution is passed to us, usually through the medium of faith. In "On the Freedom of a Christian," Martin Luther uses the imagery of marriage to suggest that everything we, the bride, own is passed over to Christ our husband by virtue of our marriage. But meanwhile, we are taken under the groom's protection, so that what is his is now ours as well. Thus our sin passes to Christ, whereas his righteousness passes to us. Under these soteriologies, there is no way around our human plight other than through what Christ's death provides.

But if we look at the theory of Abelard, we see different possibilities. Our problems are resolved through the revelation that we receive in and through Christ. The nineteenth century saw a resurgence of this soteriology, particularly under the impact of biblical studies. Whereas previously the primary focus had been on the death and resurrection of Christ, biblical scholarship focused on the importance of Jesus' life. Scholar after scholar sought "the historical Jesus," often drawing a portrait of Jesus that reflected the current nineteenth-century ideal of what it is to be human.[9] To understand Jesus' humanity was to understand what we ourselves are called to be. *In His Steps*, by Charles Sheldon, was an immensely popular late-nineteenth century book based on this thesis.[10] Meanwhile, the emphasis on Jesus' life also brought to light the social impact of his preaching of the Reign of God. Modeling oneself on the revelation given through Jesus had implications for how we are to live as a church in society. This was hardly a novel insight—Christianity from its inception had radical implications for how Christians and the church as a whole should live within society. But in a sense, the soteriological focus was historically on life after death. The reemergence of a revelational soteriology in the nineteenth century changed the focus to life here and now in the continuous creation of human history. The question became, given the revelation of God in human history, How should we live?

The point is that a revelational soteriology, unlike the other three soteriologies, is not necessarily exclusive. The revelation comes in Christ by the grace of God. But what God reveals depends upon God. In principle, there is no reason why God cannot reveal whenever, and however, and wherever God chooses. It is this notion that we will now explore.

Saving Grace: A Pluralistic Soteriology

Abelard's soteriology, and those similar to his developed in the nine-teenth and twentieth centuries, became known as the "moral example" theory of salvation. Weaknesses perceived in this theory were that too much depended upon our own actions: How is it "saving grace" if all that happens is our own decision to follow an example? Given the problem of sin, are we even *capable* of following such an example? And is God's work in our salvation limited simply to showing us what we should do? Compared to the mighty work of salvation through vicarious suffering, an Abelardian theory of salvation seemed namby-pamby indeed.

But now we know that we live in a relational world, where deepest knowledge isn't something that we see externally, and then dutifully copy, all on our own. To the contrary, knowledge occurs through the transmis-sion of energy from one event to another. As that energy is internalized, it has the capacity to transform the receiver. Knowledge is power. Reconsider the impact of Christ in a thoroughly relational world.

In chapter 3, "Radical Incarnation," we discussed God's presence in the world. Incarnation is accomplished to the extent that one responds to God's guidance by incorporating this guidance into the becoming self. We presume that God continuously guided Jesus to manifest the nature of God—the love of God—as adapted to the nature of first-century Palestine. As Jesus fully conformed himself to these aims, Jesus became the manifestation of God in history. He unfailingly responded to people and situations according to the love of God. Even on the cross, he was faithful, responding to hatred, callousness, and grief in love. He did not curse his crucifiers; rather, he prayed for them. He did not concentrate so much on his own suffering that he ignored that of those who were nailed to crosses beside him; rather, he offered comfort. He was not so absorbed in his own pain that he forgot responsibilities to family and friends; rather, he committed them to one another's care. In life and death, he was a powerful embodiment of the unfailing love of God, ever adapted to our circumstances, leading us toward communal good.

The power of this life and death is not wrapped up in Jesus alone, but in the conviction that in his life and death, we see the nature of God revealed. God is a consistent and insistent drive toward love, so much so that we say God *is* love.

To consider God incarnationally is to think of God continuously act-ing from love, luring the world toward its good through the means of ever newly given guidance. But God works in a relational world, where God's guidance necessarily interacts with the power of the past actual world in influencing each becoming moment. We are not affected by the world alone, nor by God alone, but by both.

See what this means relative to the revelation of God in Jesus. Because God is manifest in Jesus, our past world contains a strong witness to the love of God. This witness in history increases the power of God's contemporary call. That is, when God's work in history combines with God's contemporary call, the force of the call increases. When we respond in faith to the witness of God in history—whether through our own reading of the texts or through our hearing of the story—that witness enters into us as a gracious invitation to conform ourselves to the new possibilities God offers us. The word of God in history recorded in the Gospels, and the word of God given in every moment, can in combination offer us empowering possibilities for our own transformation toward love. This is saving grace.

But in a relational world, saving grace is "invitational." In John Wesley's words, it is "resistible grace." God's word to us makes it possible for us to live lives of love, but the actualization of the possibility depends upon our own response. We have the power to conform to the possibility either fully or in part, or to reject the possibility altogether. This is why the response of faith is so important. Faith is a name for the positive response to the call of God. Apart from this positive response, we create ourselves according to less loving modes of existence. Grace—the word given both in the witness of the gospel to Jesus Christ and in God's contemporary call—makes faith possible. The response of faith makes the work of grace actual in our lives, and empowers our own transformations toward love and the communal good.

And Pluralism?

God saves us in and through the revealing power of God in Jesus Christ. But there is no inherent need for any revelation of God to be exclusive. To the contrary, to the extent that a revelation is exclusive, then paradoxically the power of the revelation is weakened. Think about it. God works in and through the conditions of history, of culture, patiently working with the world toward the world's good. But given the diversity of cultures, a revelation given in one culture is not necessarily salvific for those living in another culture. If God only shows the love of

God in Western culture, never adapting that love to other cultures, then to that extent God's love is limited. But this is a contradiction to the love of God! If God saves us through revealing love under the conditions of humanity, then in principle God can reveal that love in a variety of ways, according to the varieties of cultures. And since God is never absent from any culture, as was argued in chapter 3, we must assume that more than one form of community is capable of revealing the love of God.

But the fact of a variety of revelations in no way lessens the importance of any one. It is *because* God adapts revelation to our condition that each form of revelation is of inestimable importance. While we humans speak of "the human race," and "humanity," and rightly maintain human kinship, the fact remains that we are each quite particular. If God only speaks to us in general, universal terms, how are we who live in very particular circumstances to hear? The love of God, to be the love of God, must be adapted to our condition. We who have responded to God through faith in Jesus Christ have responded to God's particular word to us. For us, there is an ultimacy and an unsurpassable sufficiency to this revelation, this word.

But one can come to God in other ways. There is nothing in this interpretation of salvation that demands that God must give the same method of salvation to all people. We have already seen that Christian soteriology has been adapted in different times and places according to different interpretations of the basic human problem. But in another culture different dimensions of the problems inherent in human existence might well emerge. In such a case, would not God work within that culture to fashion modes of redemption uniquely suited to persons in that culture? *That* we come to God rests with God's grace, given in diverse ways through many cultures; *how* we come to God rests with the very diversity of those ways, and our own responses, through which history is cumulatively created.

And Sin?

Soteriologies are always named relative to a particular understanding of that which is wrong with the human condition. Within Christianity, the naming of that wrong has been "sin." Given our ignorance of reproductive processes for so many centuries, we accounted for the pervasiveness of sin through the figure of Adam. The value of this naming is that it indicated the reality that sin somehow precedes us; we do not each make it up all by ourselves.

We do not need a historic first human being who "falls" to account for this sense of sin preceding us. Sin is always a failure to act according to the love of God in our particular circumstances. In another book I have given a full-length treatment of "original sin" as that which precedes us, bending us willy-nilly against inclusive good.[11] The evolutionary urge toward self-preservation is itself a good, but it entails a wariness of those not immediately associated with ourselves or those with whom we identify. This wariness easily becomes violence toward those perceived as "different." As societies emerge, these societies create protections for those of its preferred kind—and few protections for those perceived as different. To this day, we inherit an instinctive tendency to distrust difference. We respond to the other not in love, but in suspicion, fear, or violence. Salvation calls for a transformation toward openness to the other, extending God's love beyond our own kind.

Closely related to this are the norms from the culture that shape our conscience. In American culture today, we flood the media with norms of violence. The acceptable responses to perceived violation of one's own well-being are to shoot or to sue. We teach this to our children through cartoons and to youth and adults through many of our films. We have also blanketed the media with norms based on perverting human sexuality into opportunities for exploitation, usually through objectifying women by reducing them to their sexuality. Women then become tools for profit, whether through sales of goods or through sales of their bodies. To grow up in American culture is to deal with cultural norms of violence, woven into us as personal norms shaping our conduct. Salvation from such sin requires a transformation of our consciences.

Thus we do not require an Adam to name sin as that which goes before us, bending us toward its own repetition. Nor do we need our presence in Adam's loins to account for our own guilt. We may indeed inherit cultural norms that work against well-being, but insofar as we adopt these norms, we reinforce them through our own power, thus becoming "Adam" or "Eve" to a next generation. We are personally guilty, responsible for the continuous shaping of our culture's norms, and for our own actions that unnecessarily work against the well-being of existence on this planet. There is ample need for saving grace!

The witness of Christianity, and of all religions, is that there is a power in the world that counteracts the powers of evil. Western religions tend to name the evil as sin; Eastern religions tend to name the evil as suffering. But both name a counterforce, albeit in quite different ways. The

Christian witness is that this counterforce is the power of God, who works in and through Jesus Christ to bring us toward a creative transformation away from reenactment of the powers of sin and evil, and toward an increasingly wide communal good. God is a God of saving grace. In a pluralistic world, it is a grace to be celebrated, and to be shared with others in mission.

Questions for Reflection and Discussion

• This chapter has named five ways of understanding what happens through Christ's crucifixion: Paul's understanding of representation and sacrifice; Augustine's dramatic theory of ransom from Satan; Anselm's "satisfaction theory," or the necessity for a God-man to satisfy our debt to God; Abelard's teaching concerning the need for Christ to teach us and to mediate for us; Luther's "substitutionary atonement," where Christ stands in for our punishment. Which of these ways is most familiar to you?

• Each one of these theories is Christian, even though each teaches something different about the event of the Cross. Also, there are numerous variations of each theory. What do you make of this variety?

• Does the same thing happen "from God's point of view" in each of the theories? That is, is there a change in God because of what happens on the Cross? Explain.

• Does the same thing happen for us in each of the theories? That is, what kind of change takes place within each theory because of our faith in Jesus Christ? Explain.

• What are the roles of Jesus' life and Jesus' resurrection in each of these theories?

• How do you think God saves us?

In the days to come,
The Mount of the LORD's House shall stand
Firm above the mountains;
And it shall tower above the hills.
The peoples shall gaze on it with joy,
And the many nations shall go and shall say:
"Come,
Let us go up to the Mount of the LORD,
To the House of the God of Jacob;
That He may instruct us in His ways,
And that we may walk in His paths."
For instruction shall come forth from Zion,
The word of the LORD from Jerusalem.
Thus He will judge among the many peoples,
And arbitrate for the multitude of nations,
However distant;
And they shall beat their swords into plowshares
And their spears into pruning hooks.
Nations shall not take up
Sword against nation;
They shall never again know war;
But [all persons] shall sit
Under [their] grapevine or fig tree
With no one to disturb [them].
For it was the LORD of Hosts who spoke.
Though all the peoples walk
Each in the names of its gods,
We will walk
In the name of the LORD our God
Forever and ever.

—Mic. 4:1-5 (TANAKH)

CHAPTER SEVEN

MISSION IN A PLURALISTIC WORLD

If God works with all the world toward its good, what purpose is left for mission activity? Should we not trust God with the well-being of other cultures, and stay with our own in some "noninterference" policy? If we choose such a course, we will be thwarting our own good, and quite likely hindering God's purposes toward a world community of many communities. I believe that God is calling us to a new and more intense form of mission activity in the world today—not to convert the world to our own religion, but to convert the world toward friendship. Religions must become friends with one another, working cooperatively with people of other religions toward deeper forms of common good. God may well be calling us to a world where friendship is the model of our mutual relatedness. In such a model, we are called to share our own story, to listen to the other's story, and to seek ways of working together to alleviate the ills of the world. We are called to be friends in our common home, the earth.

If we believe that God is at work in the world, and if we love God, then we will care about the various works of God. And my ultimate conviction is that God is leading us each beyond our religious isolation and fear of one another toward a new way of being community—a community of communities, each with its uniqueness, and therefore each with its rich contribution to the world's good. Only as we interact with one another in friendship can such a community of communities come to pass.

Mission As Friendship

" 'You are My friends,' " said Jesus in John's Gospel, " 'if you do what I command you. . . . This I command you, that you love one another' " (15:14, 17). How are we to love one another if we do not know one another? A major task of missions, then, is to share who we are with one another, so that we might enter into the model of mission as cooperative friendship. Apart from knowledge of one another's convictions and concerns, we remain strangers to one another, subject to stereotyping and dismissal.

I remember my own first living encounter with Buddhism. I was a new Ph.D., trained in Western philosophy in general and process theology/philosophy in particular, when I was invited to teach introductory courses in Eastern religions at a state university. In studying Buddhism I was struck with parallels between process philosophy and Buddhist philosophy—so much so that when I was invited to participate in a Buddhist/process dialogue in Hawaii, I eagerly accepted.

The first night of the conference involved a reception at a Tendai Buddhist temple—my first visit to a sacred space that was neither Christian nor Jewish! I went with much curiosity. We were received graciously into a large and simple hall, and I noticed a doorway leading to gardens beyond the hall. So I went through the doorway, marveling at the lovely simplicity of the gardens, where stones were mingled with plantings—and then I saw the image! It was a statue of the Buddha, approximately nine feet high. The Buddha looked like a man except that he had numerous arms, spreading like a halo all around him! In each hand was a different instrument. Had I not been studying Buddhism, I'd have seen the image only as an idol. But because I'd been studying, I knew what was represented. Each hand symbolized a different way of compassion and wisdom by which the Buddha reaches us. The many hands and tools showed that whatever your need, the Buddha would meet your condition in order to help you along the road toward enlightenment. The image— large, imposing, and benevolent—bespoke the Buddha's infinite wisdom in knowing our need, and compassion in meeting our need. My study of Buddhism had led to respect and appreciation, making friendship possible. I eagerly entered into the dialogue.

Several things follow from taking friendship as a model. Friends are usually people who discover that they share something in common, despite their differences. Those differences do not diminish the friendship, they enrich it. For example, I could discuss God's compassion with a Christian friend, and we would each have an implicit understanding of the other. We tend to think of God's compassion as exemplified in Jesus Christ, through whom God meets our need and brings us to wholeness, or salvation. Because of God's compassion to us, we are to be compassionate to one another. Discussion of compassion with a Buddhist gives different insight.

The Lotus Sutra gives many parables illustrating the Buddha's compassion. It is like a rain that falls on many kinds of plants, and while each plant receives the same rain, each responds according to its own kind, and this is right and good. Or the Buddha's compassion can be illustrated through a humble monk called "Not Despising," who renders honor to every person regardless of that person's attitude toward him, for "Not Despising" sees in each person the potential for Buddhahood. Seeing that potential contributes toward eliciting that potential. Or the Buddha is like a father luring his children from a burning house by offering them playthings that they want, just to lure them away from danger. But once they have responded by running out of the burning house, the father gives them not the foolish playthings they desire, but that which truly meets their deeper need. Compassion understood in a Buddhist context differs from compassion understood in a Christian context, but in ways that supplement it.

The reverse is also so. For a Buddhist to hear from a Christian about the compassion of God supplements and enriches Buddhist understanding. Friendship does not then require that the Buddhist leave the centrality of Buddhist insight, nor that Christians leave the centrality of Christian insight—only that, hearing the other, they each respect the other, learn from the other, and so deepen their previous understanding. A Christian might say, "Ah! So this is how God works in and through Buddhist teaching!" And of course the Buddhist might say, "So! The Buddha even uses Christianity as a tool to lead some toward eventual enlightenment!" We each perceive the other in and through the veil of our own understanding. But our own understanding is enlarged and enriched. Mutual understanding can enhance each form of religion in ways we are barely beginning to appreciate.

In and through differences, friends have something to learn from each other; they are not clones, they are friends. Friendship requires an honesty that dares to share the depths of one's self with the other. Friends also join in activities meaningful to both, sometimes simply from the enjoyment of being together, and at other times in order to accomplish mutual goals. Friends rejoice in each other's good fortune, and grieve over misfortune. Fundamentally, friends respect each other's personhood, and trust each other, knowing that each cares about the other's well-being. Finally, in and through friendship there is the possibility of transformation. Each takes the other's concerns into the self, and in caring for the friend, finds one's own horizons enlarged. Friendship is an adventure in becoming a communal self.

For example, I have a friend whose own disability has made her an advocate for all persons who go through life dealing with some form of disabling condition. "Disabling" is actually "differently abling," since persons who lack abilities common to most people develop their own unique ways of exercising their personhood within community. She also spent seven years in ministry among the deaf and hearing impaired. Because of my friendship with her, I myself have become much more sensitive to issues of this nature. I am now far more aware of speech patterns that stereotype deafness or disabilities, and I join her in advocating accessibility. Through friendship, her concerns have become my concerns as well, even though our actual experience of disabilities is quite different. Friendship builds upon differences to create common interests, common work.

John B. Cobb Jr. points out that if we truly engage in the activity of mutual understanding—what I am calling becoming friends—then we well might find ourselves changing. If we think about relations after the model of friendship, then we must agree with him. To become a friend to someone is to take that person's concerns into oneself, to learn to empathize with that friend, and to share one's deepest self to whatever extent possible in the friendship. But to so empathize with another is, in a relational world, to be changed to some extent by this relation. We exist in a flow of relation; we do not stay precisely the same from moment to moment. In and through our responses to the influences upon us, we create ourselves again and again. There is a conjoining of interests that affects the ongoing development of our selves.

When we form friendships across religious lines or cultural lines or both, we open ourselves to being influenced by perceptions and concerns that were formerly alien to us. We become open to enlarged understandings, to which we respond not only by how we act, but by who we are. Thus, mission after the model of friendship invites us all into interreligious dialogue, but in such dialogue, there is no guarantee as to how we will and will not continue to become ourselves. Dialogue calls for our deepening trust in the ever present guidance of God. Through such trust, we can dare openness to the other, knowing that God will infuse that openness with God's own loving guidance.

Precisely because mission as friendship holds open the possibility of unexpected modes of our own transformation, it is essential that we have a strong sense of our own religious identity. This is not for the sake of holding on to it for dear life, as if we cannot possibly let it go. Rather, it is for the sake of sharing who we are as fully as possible. To speak of Christ requires that we take the trouble to know who Christ has been not only for ourselves, but for Christians throughout history. We must know our own tradition as fully as possible if we are to share it. Dialogue can send us to history books to find out just why we believe this or that, and to theology books for various opinions on what this can mean for us today. Ultimately, of course, we must query our own experience: How do we discern the work of God in Christ within ourselves and our own communities? Mission as friendship demands that we know who we are and have been as Christians.

Friendship As Mission: Local

What would happen if friendship were applied to religious pluralism, particularly at congregational levels? Imagine that an Islamic mosque and a United Methodist church exist in the same town. An attitude of friendship toward each other would encourage each to learn more about the other. Some of this learning could be through introductory books that each might recommend to the other. Perhaps each community would start study groups dealing with the other's religion, looking not only at books giving the history and beliefs of the religion, but also at the major texts—the Koran for the one, the New Testament for the other. But most of the learning would be through conversations designed to share oneself with another so that the other might know who we really are, and how and why we understand God as we do.

But to engage in such conversation, of course, requires that we have a pretty good self-understanding! The Methodists would also have to learn more about what it means to be a Christian who is Methodist. Perhaps they would begin to study Methodist hymns, or read some of John Wesley's writings, and become more acquainted with the connectional structure of their church. But they could not stop there; they would have to delve into Christian history as a whole, and in doing so, they would discover the vibrancy that marks the development of Christian beliefs. They would learn that contemporary forms of faith are not exactly the same as earlier forms, even when the same language is used. To be a Christian is to be involved in a continuous adventure with God within the context of shifting cultures. Methodists who are concerned to share who they are with those of another faith would feel themselves bound to know more about who they are, who they have been, and who they might yet be. The same, of course, would be true of the Islamic community. To share one's story with another is to be able to speak personally about what it means to be a Muslim, or a Methodist.

To share oneself with another in friendship is to listen to the other's story. True, we tell our own story so that the other might know us more fully, but if friendship is the model, the other must also speak from the depths of what it is to be Muslim. There would be questions each would ask of the other, and some of them might be embarrassing: "Do you really eat a body during what you call Communion?" "Do you really have warfare as a pillar of your faith?" Friends dare to ask each other the hard things—and to answer them.

Becoming friends means to share a meal together. Perhaps the Methodists would host the Muslims for a church supper, or perhaps the Muslims might invite the Methodists to participate in one of their feasts. Dining together, people talk about familial concerns, and also branch out into common concerns about conditions in their town or city. Perhaps they would discover that Muslim children experience discrimination in the schools, and the Methodists would go to bat for the Muslims to see that there is greater respect for different religions among school children. Perhaps they would discover a mutual concern about the wanton violence in so many films, and together they could devise ways to respond to this. Perhaps they would discern a need in the town for fairer labor practices, or better housing for the poor, or better care for the elderly, and join forces to address the identified problem.

In the process, each congregation might discover unique virtues to be admired in the other—virtues peculiarly associated with the other faith. Perhaps there could be ways to approximate some of these virtues in one's own community of faith in ways consonant with one's faith. Paradoxically, growing in these virtues does not make each congregation less than itself, but more deeply itself as it makes choices concerning its own development in its faith. Interreligious dialogue at the congregational level can deepen one's own religious faith, even in and through learning about another. The Methodists might marvel at the grace of God that they perceive at work within the Islamic context, and praise God the more for God's universal care. Friendship does not require that each become the other, only that each offer oneself to the other and be willing to receive from the other, toward the common good.

Friendship As Mission: Global

And what of sending people to other lands? Would this still be necessary in a pluralistic world? I maintain that this is essential. Globally, we live in a world where economics weave the peoples of the world together for good and for ill—and for far too many, the bent is toward the ill. Economic worth replaces quality of life, wreaking havoc with sustainable lifestyles. We live in a world plagued by hatred of difference, and by violence in all forms: warfare, greed, exploitation, and abuse. We live in a world where the means of communication provide near instantaneous knowledge—or distorted knowledge—about what is happening in countries across the globe. And we live in a world where environmental destruction and greenhouse gases threaten the well-being of the planet itself, along with all life upon it. In such a world, any reluctance to engage in mission as friendship is not only a violation of friendship, it is sin. It allows the enmities of this world to continue unchecked. Not to engage religiously in global friendship is to cede the world to forces of evil.

For example, if religion is a potent way by which God draws the world into forms of community, it is the greatest of travesties that religion has been used as a catalyst for terrorism, warfare, and destruction of the common good. But religion *is* used in such a way—religion against religion, and even sect against sect within an otherwise common religion! Christianity itself is a sorry witness to this, not only historically, but also in the present day as Catholics and Protestants torment each other, particularly in Northern Ireland. Granted, the political issues are broader than the religious issues, but religion becomes the icon that blesses the warfare in the name of the sacred. In our own recent American history, we have experienced this most horrifically through the terrorism of September 11. While a variety of factors—the plight of Palestinians and the results of global economics—undoubtedly contributed to this vicious attack, Islam was used to bless the attack. American Muslims in particular agonized not only at the losses of September 11, but also over such an egregious misuse of Islam on the part of the terrorist extremists. Using religion to bless violence is a travesty striking at the heart of religion everywhere.

Friendship as global mission, then, must take place not only by seeking a knowledge of one another, but by together seeking deeper knowledge of the roots of the ills that plague our planet. An exemplary Buddhist group in Japan, the Rissho Kosei-kai, illustrates the possibilities of mission as friendship in a global context. This branch of Tendai Buddhism was founded in the 1930s. Convinced that the Buddha is "skillful in means" and therefore is more than competent to see to the world's religious movement toward enlightenment, these Buddhists decided that their unique task would be acts of compassion to alleviate the world's ills. Further, since the world's ills span every country, continent, and religious group, to address those ills requires interreligious cooperation. And so the Rissho Kosei-kai have, since its beginnings, worked with leaders of religions around the world to influence the political leaders of the world toward peace. They have also been among the first to enter countries decimated by warfare to tend to the suffering, particularly looking to the needs of those who are least able to care for themselves, the young and the aged. In the process of doing good, the Rissho Kosei-kai have indeed shared their Buddhist beliefs. If persons decide that this form of belief meets their own religious need, the Rissho Kosei-kai gladly welcome them into their community. But conversion is not their mission; compassion is their mission.

In my experience, persons who are most open to Christian affirmation of other religions are often those persons who have spent their lives working in the midst of other religions. What may have begun as an effort simply to convert others to Christianity often seems to have become an effort to work with people toward their own communal well-being. I recently heard a retired Methodist missionary from Chile speak about the agricultural college The United Methodist Church founded in the desert of northern Chile. Its purpose? Caught between war and famine, mountain people were leaving their homes and traveling to the cities in order to find work, but in the cities they found themselves the "lowest of the low," exploited and beaten. The agricultural college shares new techniques of mountain farming methods with the people so that they can live productively on the land they love. Since the establishment of the college in 1992, the flow of the people to the cities has decreased. The purpose of the mission was to work with the people toward their own well-being. Christian identity was not hidden, any more than is Buddhist identity in Rissho Kosei-kai. But Christian identity pushed beyond its own replication, and into the creative transformation of the lives of the people it served.

The missionaries responsible for this work did not fear others, nor were they ignorant or unappreciative of the beliefs of the Chileans. Their own theologies did not require that others first conform to Christian beliefs in order to be loved by God. To the contrary, they were convinced that God loved the Chileans whether the missionaries were there or not, and that God worked with the Chileans toward their own well-being, whether or not the missionaries were there. The missionaries' self-understanding was gratitude at the privilege of being partners with God and with the Chilean people in contributing to the common good. A theology of affirmation is a powerful catalyst for working together toward the communal good.

Hans Küng, Roman Catholic theologian, has been instrumental in bringing persons from the world's religions together with world political leaders (in this case, former heads of state) for the sake of developing a common ethic. Together, the religious and political leaders created a document agreeing on shared concerns for the common good. The former heads of state share this document with present heads of state, arguing for its consideration in all political decisions. Such documents play an important role, but naming a common ethic involves more than documents; it requires joint action to bring about those things named as the common good.

" 'You are My friends,' said Jesus, 'if you do what I command you . . . love one another.' " Is there not ample ground within Christianity to exercise this love not simply among the like-minded, but throughout the world? Within our own tradition there is the model of giving a cup of cold water in the name of Christ to those who thirst. Notice the two elements: the actual cup of water, which meets the physical need, and the name of Christ, which makes clear the name of the one through whom the cup is given. Christians are not to minister to the needs of the world anonymously, but in the name of Christ, through whom God has shown compassion toward us. But one does not give the cup in order to proclaim the name of Christ; to the contrary, one gives the cup because Christ compels us to love the other, and the other needs the cup. When we say in whose name we give it, we say this not in order to convert, so that the other will become like us in belief. Rather, we say Christ's name to explain why we give this cup. Conversion may be a by-product of our ministry, but in the deepest sense, we leave conversion to God. Our immediate concern is care for the one in need.

This illustration suggests a one-on-one ministry, but this cannot be the whole of it. The problems creating havoc with our common good are not one-on-one problems. They are systemic problems arising from largely materialistic economic approaches to the world. Mission as friendship at this level takes on wonderful possibilities. There is an old saying that one "fights fire with fire." I know this image well! I lived for a time at the edge of the foothills of Southern California, and just beyond our home the mountains rose steeply, filled with grasses and chaparral. In one hot October an arsonist set a fire in the foothills about ten miles beyond us, though ten miles is nothing to those flames. They quickly spread, leaping from one mountain to another! The firefighters not only fought the flames with aerial drops, they also started another fire that would burn toward the first fire. When the two forces of flame met, there was nothing left to consume, and the fire died out.

Systemic forces that wreak evil are too much for a single individual to fight, although individuals do indeed become catalysts to unite a new social force against the evil. But religious organizations are themselves systemic forces. The church, through its national headquarters and through its coalitions, such as the National Council of Churches, can itself be an intensification of Christian witness, and a powerful force toward the good. It can be the fire that fights the fire of evil. Local churches who themselves engage in interreligious friendships can intensify the work of friendship in and through their support of their denominations and larger Christian groupings. To do so, the local churches must support mission as friendship.

Global mission then takes place through missionaries who devote themselves to God in ministry around the globe, participating in the corporate actions of the institutional church. In and through the witness of the church, God will convert some to Christianity. But such growth is a by-product of mission, not the main goal of mission. The church's main goal is to serve God through its friendship with other religions, and through cooperative work to analyze the world's ills and act together to alleviate those ills.

And What of Clashing Differences?

Friends discover their points of irreducible disagreement as well as their points of agreement. To increase in knowledge of the other is to realize that the differences go deep. There is not necessarily agreement on what constitutes the ills of the world, or even why those ills exist. This simply reflects the reality that the religions of the world are not reducible to one another; friendship does not mean sameness, it means a commitment to respect the other in difference, and to work with the other in areas of common agreement.

Differences are social, and not simply conceptual. For example, all of the religions of the world have placed women as a class in secondary positions within society. One of the strong marks of Western Christianity has been a change in the subordination of women, particularly in the past two centuries. Through Christian influence, some of the more egregious harms done to women in the name of patriarchy have been modified. But of course, even in saying this, I must recognize that what I call "harm" is not necessarily called harm by others, not even the women affected by that which I name "harm." Disagreements among religions, and of course even within religions, are real, and these disagreements have social consequences. How does this affect mission as friendship? Do Christians quietly accept what they identify as deleterious practices in the name of "difference" and "respect"?

Again, consider the model of friendship. Friends do not always agree. In fact, friendship can entail severe differences of opinion and practice. Friends can be very good at arguing with each other. And sometimes the differences become bitter, and friendships die because of intransigence (whether perceived or real) on important issues. But when the latter occurs, there is real loss.

In interreligious friendships at the institutional, congregational, and personal levels, differences will naturally be identified, and there will be times when those differences seem nonnegotiable. The model of a working friendship means that these differences will be faced honestly, and the groups will work hard not necessarily to eliminate the differences, but at least to understand each other's position. In the process, there may well be passionate arguments against or for certain beliefs and practices. Friendship prefers honest and open disagreement to a shallow avoidance of naming the places of disagreement. Further, every religion stands within a moving stream of its own tradition; no tradition ever stands still (unless, of course, it dies, in which case its only change is its slow decay). Religions can legitimately seek to influence each other in directions each perceives as positive. The underlying rule is respect for the other's own decisions concerning the issue at hand, a commitment to the friendship itself, and a commitment to work together in areas of agreement concerning the mutually perceived common good. Good friends do not allow the disagreements to end the friendship.

The citation from Micah that begins this chapter speaks of a vision of what has often been called, "The Peaceable Kingdom." We meet this vision as well in the second chapter of Isaiah. In Isaiah, however, the section ends with "Nation shall not take up Sword against nation; They shall never again know war" (v. 4 *TANAKH*). The chapter then goes on to call Israel to walk in the light of the Lord, speaking of the treasure that will follow their obedience. But in Micah the text about "The Peaceable Kingdom" ends like this:

> Though all the peoples walk
> Each in the names of its gods,
> We will walk
> In the name of the LORD our God
> Forever and ever. (v. 5 *TANAKH*)

Like the Isaiah text, Micah speaks of all the nations of the world streaming to Mt. Zion in order to learn the ways of God, which are just. But Micah emphasizes more than Isaiah the interesting fact that the people return to their own place, bringing with them the knowledge gained from Israel's God. Because of this knowledge, they change their ways in directions of peace: "Nation shall not take up Sword against nation; They shall never again know war; But [all persons] shall sit Under [their] grapevine or fig tree With no one to disturb [them]" (4:3*b*-4 *TANAKH*).

What the Micah text adds is the interesting phrase quoted above. The nations have indeed learned the ways of peace from Mt. Zion, but they continue to follow their own religions. In today's language, they entered into dialogue, and were changed by the dialogue, even while they remained themselves. And the Jews in the text likewise remain themselves, more deeply than ever: "We will walk In the name of the LORD our God Forever and ever" (4:5 *TANAKH*).

This ancient text speaks today about the possibilities of mission as friendship, working together toward today's longings for a "peaceable kingdom" where the nations never again will train for war. To regard the religious other as "friend" involves us in mission together, sharing who we are, and working together for the common good. Being most deeply who we are, we are open to God's transformative call toward how we might yet be. In such openness toward the other and toward the common good, "we will walk In the name of the LORD our God forever and ever."

Questions for Reflection and Discussion

- What arguments can you make for thinking of mission as primarily for the purpose of converting persons to belief in Jesus Christ?

- Is belief in Jesus Christ weakened if others do not come to God through him? Why or why not?

- Discuss the possibility that whereas the early days of mission were aimed toward conversion, God's call now might be toward mission as friendship. What is gained? What is lost?

- How do we discern God's call? That is, if God is really calling us in these directions, how would we "know" it?

- We have often understood "preaching the gospel to every creature" as a call to words leading to conversion. But "preaching the gospel" involves how we live as well as what we say. Discuss how mission as friendship is faithful to the Great Commission.

- Is the vision of the religions of the world leading the world to become a community of diverse communities, living toward the common good, *too* visionary? Surely the Micah text was not descriptive of eighth-century Israel; why should we use it as a vision for today? What is the role of vision in our Christian lives anyhow?

- How would you formulate the imperatives of mission in a religiously pluralistic world?

NOTES

Chapter 1. The Task

1. See Jacques Dupuis, *Toward a Christian Theology of Religious Pluralism* (Maryknoll: Orbis, 1997) for a fuller discussion of this history.

2. See especially Cobb's book, *Beyond Dialogue: Toward a Mutual Transformation of Christianity and Buddhism* (Eugene, Ore.: Wipf and Stock Publishers, 1998).

3. Paul F. Knitter, *No Other Name: A Critical Survey of Christian Attitudes Toward the World Religions* (Maryknoll: Orbis, 1985); *One Earth, Many Religions: Multifaith Dialogue and Global Responsibility* (Maryknoll: Orbis, 1995); Jesus and the Other Names: Christian Mission and Global Responsibility (Maryknoll: Orbis, 1996).

4. Hick's first book dealing with pluralism was *God and the Universe of Faiths*, rev. ed. (London: Fount Paperbacks, 1977). A more recent book is *A Christian Theology of Religions: A Rainbow of Faiths* (Louisville: Westminster/John Knox, 1995).

Chapter 2. Creation

1. Sarvepalli Radhakrishnan and Charles A. Moore, ed., *A Source Book in Indian Philosophy* (Princeton, N.J.: Princeton University Press, 1957).

2. Alfred North Whitehead, *Process and Reality: An Essay in Cosmology*, corrected edition, ed. David Ray Griffin and Donald W. Sherburne (New York: The Free Press, 1978).

3. For example, see Rolf P. Knierim, *The Task of Old Testament Theology: Substance, Method, and Cases: Essays* (Grand Rapids: Eerdmans, 1995), especially 186-91, and Jon D. Levenson, *Creation and the Persistence of Evil: The Jewish Drama of Divine Omnipotence* (Princeton, N.J.: Princeton University Press, 1994), particularly chapter 2.

4. C. S. Lewis, *The Magician's Nephew* (New York: HarperCollins, 1994).

Chapter 3. Radical Incarnation

1. Wing-tsit Chan, comp. and ed., *A Source Book in Chinese Philosophy* (Princeton, N.J.: Princeton University Press, 1963), 146.

2. I first developed this summary of James's position in "Pragmatic Pluralism," a lecture I delivered in 1998 at the Highlands Institute for Religious and Philosophic Thought. The lecture was included in *Religion in a Pluralistic Age: Proceedings of the Third International Conference on Philosophical Theology*, ed. Donald A. Crosby and Charley D. Hardwick (New York: Peter Lang, 2001). Relevant portions of that lecture are repeated here, with permission from Peter Lang Publishing, Inc.

3. William James, *Essays in Radical Empiricism [and] A Pluralistic Universe*, ed. Ralph Barton Perry (New York: E. P. Dutton, 1971).

4. One is reminded of George Lindbeck's definition of Christian doctrine as a system of grammar governing the construction of Christian life. See *The Nature of Doctrine: Religion and Philosophy in a Postliberal Age* (Philadelphia: Westminster, 1984).

5. R. S. Sugirtharajah, ed., *Asian Faces of Jesus* (Maryknoll: Orbis, 1993).

Chapter 4. The Image of God

1. Arthur J. Arberry, trans. *The Koran Interpreted* (London: Allen & Unwin Ltd.; New York: Macmillan, 1955).

2. Augustine, *Concerning the City of God Against the Pagans*, trans. Henry Bettenson (Hammondsworth: Penguin, 1972), Book XI, Section 28.

3. Anselm of Canterbury, Monologium, in *Basic Writings*, trans. S. N. Deane (LaSalle, Ill.: Open Court Publishing Co., 1962), chapter LXVII, 178.

4. See, for example, Thomas's articles on the image of God in Question XCIII of *Summa Theologica*.

5. Martin Luther, *Works*, XLII.47, commentary on Genesis, ed. Jaroslav Pelikan (St. Louis: Concordia, 1955), 62-64.

6. John Wesley, *A Plain Account of Christian Perfection*, new ed. (London: Epworth Press, 1968).

7. "Come, O Thou Traveler Unknown," *The United Methodist Hymnal* (Nashville: The United Methodist Publishing House, 1989), 386.

8. In the introduction I cited the work of Paul Knitter, who argues that the call to all religions to work together toward justice is the basis and goal of religious pluralism. Obviously I sympathize with Knitter's judgment, but base it theologically in the image of God.

9. "Holy, Holy, Holy! Lord God Almighty," *The United Methodist Hymnal* (Nashville: The United Methodist Publishing House, 1989), 64.

Chapter 5. The Reign of God

1. Paul Reps and Nyogen Senzaki, comp. *Zen Flesh, Zen Bones: A Collection of Zen and Pre-Zen Writings* (Boston: Charles E. Tuttle Co., 1957), 35.

2. This point was stressed by my colleague, Amy-Jill Levine, Carpenter Professor of New Testament Studies at Vanderbilt Divinity School.

3. Jay McDaniel, *With Roots and Wings: Christianity in an Age of Ecology and Dialogue* (Maryknoll: Orbis, 1998).

Chapter 6. Saving Grace

1. Aristotle, *Generation of Animals*, 1.II, XX.

2. As Augustine says: "[Christ] was not in the loins of Adam." See *The Literal Meaning of Genesis*, trans. and annotated John Hammond Taylor (New York: Newman Press, 1982), 10.19.

3. See John Dominic Crossan's account of this in *The Historical Jesus: The Life of a Mediterranean Jewish Peasant* (San Francisco: HarperSanFrancisco, 1991), especially 383-87. See also Gregory J. Riley, *Resurrection Reconsidered: Thomas and John in Controversy* (Minneapolis: Fortress, 1995), 16. In this book and again in *The River of God: A New History of Christian Origins* (San Francisco: HarperSanFrancisco, 2001), Riley gives a detailed account of the evolution of "resurrection" in ancient Middle Eastern cultures.

4. See Joachim Jeremias, *New Testament Theology* (New York: Scribner, 1971), 298.

5. Gustaf Aulén describes three main types of the idea of the atonement in *Christus Victor* (New York: Macmillan, 1969). See also Riley's *River of God* for a discussion of Hellenic influences on early Christian soteriologies.

6. See Elaine Pagels, *The Origin of Satan* (New York: Random House, 1995) for a history of the idea of Satan.

7. Anselm of Canterbury, *Cur Deus Homo* (eleventh century).

8. See Abelard's *Theologia Christiana*.

9. Albert Schweitzer wrote *The Quest of the Historical Jesus* (Minneapolis: Fortress, 2001), in order to debunk these imposed ideals, and to show that the real Jesus was an apocalyptic preacher totally different from any nineteenth-century portrait.

10. Charles Sheldon, *In His Steps*, ed. Harold J. Chadwick (North Brunswick, N.J.: Bridge-Logos Publishers, 2000). There are reflections of this sensitivity in the contemporary "What Would Jesus Do?" movement.

11. Marjorie Hewitt Suchocki, *The Fall to Violence: Original Sin in Relational Theology* (New York: Continuum, 1994).